# Mozarthaus Vienna

Mozarthaus Vienna

and

WIEN MUSEUM
MOZARTWOHNUNG

# TABLE OF CONTENTS

*"... the building
with two facades on
Domgasse and Schulerstrasse*

HOTEL

# Mozarthaus Vienna

*"Representative, upmarket apartment, central location, piano nobile, 4 rooms, 2 closets, annual rent of 450 guldens plus costs"*

## FROM THE "FIGAROHAUS"
## TO THE MOZARTHAUS VIENNA

Impressive at the time for its four stories and attic
conversion, the building with two facades on Domgasse 5
and Schulerstrasse 8 was a desirable address in Vienna
even in Mozart's day. Originally only a two-story building,
it acquired its present appearance in 1716 under its then
owner, the respectable master builder Andrea Simone
Carove. On his death a year later, the house passed to
his son-in-law, Albert Camesina, who had made a name
for himself as a stuccoist at the Viennese court. When
the Mozarts moved in, the house belonged to Camesina's
widowed daughter-in-law Maria Anna, who, as a pre-
caution, had entered the names of her two underage sons,
Joseph and Albert, into the land register as future heirs.

According to Imperial tax records, the annual rent for
the "four rooms, 2 closets, kitchen, attic, basement, 2 fire-
wood stores" was 450 guldens. The sum of 480 guldens
has come down to us from Leopold Mozart, so his estimate
was fairly accurate. The Mozarts moved in on September
29, 1784; the six members of the household quit the
expensive Schulerstrasse apartment on April 23, 1787. The
Camesina family sold the house a few years later. From

1799, it belonged to the portrait painter Johann Baptist Lampi senior, then his children. Thereafter the line of ownership becomes unclear because the property changed hands several times. It is now no longer possible to say when the Mozarts' apartment was subdivided. What is verifiable, however, is that even the living room in Schulerstrasse was occasionally subdivided, and that the opening of a shop caused the entrance to be moved from Schulerstraße to Domgasse, where the sole entrance to the property remains to this day.

On the occasion of the 150th anniversary of Mozart's death in 1941, competent offices in the City of Vienna were given the task of establishing a memorial in the "Figarohaus". Initially comprising only three rooms – the entrance area off the stair as well as the two rooms overlooking Schulerstrasse – it was opened on November 28 by the Nazi politician Baldur von Schirach during the "German Reich's Mozart Week". Even after alterations were carried out in 1965, the former apartment remained divided into three parts, the memorial and two private apartments. It was not until 1976 that the Museums of the City of Vienna had the opportunity to lease all the rooms that once formed the Mozart apartment and to restore its original layout.

The concepts underlying the exhibitions and the manner in which they were realized within the memorial reflected the spirit of the age. When the memorial was re-installed in 1951, the hero worship of the Nazi years was revised. The then curator, Franz Glück, sought "to remove from these rooms everything that is a reflection of a particular age, everything that smacks of emotionalism,

and to create a kind of miniature museum using the few items that are still available" (Foreword to *Der Mozart-Erinnerungsraum*, 1953). The exhibitions in the memorial were long characterized by a historicizing view of Mozart and his age. As there are none of Mozart's personal possessions in the present-day collections of Wien Museum, pieces of late 18th-century furniture were used as substitutes to recreate the spirit of the place. There was a break with this outdated practice in the mid-1990s when the

musicians' memorials managed by Wien Museum set about attracting new visitor groups and musicians' former homes were re-designed by Elsa Prochazka along identical lines. The architect produced a design that consciously avoided reconstruction. She replaced Mozart's lost furniture with pieces redolent of his era. They "fill the spaces formerly occupied by the maestro's possessions and convey to visitors the sounds, texts, music and images that will hopefully enable them to recreate in their imaginations the spirits of the people who lived and worked there" (Pochazka, 1996).

Even when Mozart's apartment re-opened most recently in 1996, the owners could not reach agreement on how to renovate the whole block.

In the course of preparations for the celebrations marking the 250th anniversary of Mozart's birth, negotiations on the future of the listed building were again held with the owner, and this time were concluded successfully. The building remains the property of the private Sucher Foundation that, on behalf of the Mozarthaus Vienna, leases Mozart's historic apartment as well as the two stories above it (they have stood empty for years) and the two basements and the ground floor with its modern entrance. Almost 1,000 m² of usable floor space is thus available to the new Mozarthaus Vienna. Technical facilities, the museum shop and other installations are housed at Domgasse 3

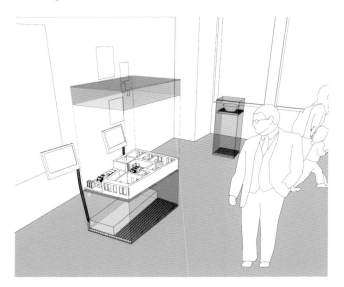

that has also been leased – in this case from the Archbish-opric of Vienna.

On behalf of the City of Vienna, Wien Holding, in conjunction with Raiffeisen Holding Wien-Niederöster-reich and Wien Museum (in whose responsibility the Mozarthaus Vienna lies) founded the Mozarthaus Vienna Errichtungs- und Betriebs GmbH that establishes and operates the new Mozart Center in line with private sector practices.

## RENOVATION OF THE BUILDING AND
## INSTALLATION OF THE MOZARTHAUS VIENNA

The Viennese architect Klaus Becker was responsible for the external refurbishment of the plain 17th century town house. Another Viennese architect, Gustav Pichelmann, converted its interior into an exhibition space and venue. Thorough surveys in conjunction with the Bundesdenkmalamt (Federal Monuments' Agency) were undertaken first and substantially influenced the program of refurbishment. The Mozarthaus Vienna has several functions. While most of its rooms are used as exhibition and museum space, there is also an events area and a service area. The top floor and the attic are private homes – the house therefore is not only a museum and still has much the same purpose it had during Mozart's time.

Visitors now enter the museum through the entrance formerly used by coaches. Its ribbed vaults have practical-

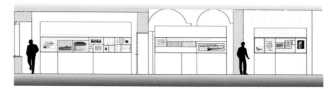

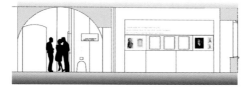

ly been untouched. The brick vaults in the basement are
of special architectural interest and have been retained.
The masonry in the lower sections of the basement
walls was in such poor condition that the Federal Monuments' Agency insisted on a wall lining of gray and white
slabs whose shades correspond to the building's refurbished gray and white exterior. The masonry above the
slabs, which conceal technical installations, has been left
exposed. Within the vaults are fitted visible acoustic
installations that allow chamber music concerts to be
held in the basement's events room. Acoustics was the
responsibility of Karl-Bernd Quiring. Also found in
the basement is a small "Mozart Learning Center" which
is intended to complement the exhibitions already on
offer upstairs.

To the right of the entrance area is the historic inner
courtyard with its typically Viennese external access decks
that have also been refurbished. As part of that work, a
bricked-up window on the ground floor was opened up
again to allow a view of the new café in the entrance area.
A glass roof was built over the inner courtyard that is now
used as the new museum's reception area. The courtyard

is included in the re-design of the museum: a display case with two screens informs visitors about Mozart's arrival in Vienna and the history of the building. An additional and highly visible element, one that fills the space from the floor to the underside of the first floor access deck, is a stela equipped with two screens that give visitors more information before their visit.

The exhibitions start on the third floor. Visitors make their way down through the building to Mozart's historic apartment on the first floor, formerly the *piano nobile*. The layout of the exhibitions on the third and second floors is almost identical to the old arrangement. Installed in each room is a display unit containing exhibits. These units appear to be of a temporary nature within the historic building.

The exhibits have been selected and placed in their historical context by Joachim Riedl. Those on the third and second floors are displayed mainly in the units. The paintings and exhibits tell the story of Mozart in Vienna and explain the background to his most important compositions. Audioguides for these exhibitions are available as is a multimedia presentation by checkpointmedia that

provides visitors with more information and enriches their experience of the collection.

The audiovisual installations in the Mozarthaus have been inspired by the technology of Mozart's day when – many decades before the invention of photography and movies – optical experiments and illusions, automatons and mechanical tricks were used to astonish theatergoers.

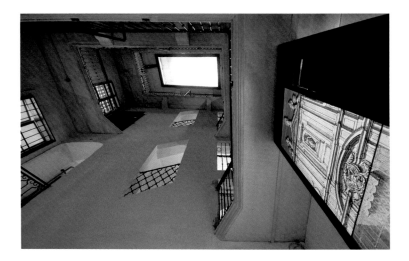

Today's new media continue that tradition and through the senses convey to visitors an impression of Mozart's life and times.

A sound and video installation in the covered courtyard prepares visitors for their tour of the Mozarthaus. The use of multimedia continues on the third floor where a flight across old Vienna shows the most important locations during Mozart's "golden years" in the city. Among them are such residences of his as:

– Wipplingerstrasse 19: While living at this address he married Constanze and composed important piano concertos;

– Domgasse 5: Where *The Marriage of Figaro* was composed;

– Währingerstrasse 26: Where the "Jupiter" symphony was composed;

– Rauhensteingasse 8: Where *The Magic Flute* and his *Requiem* were composed and where Mozart died.

Small peep shows and a panoramic projection illustrating the famous "Grabennymphen" (prostitutes who plied their trade on Graben) reveal one of the seamier aspects of life in 18th-century Vienna. Combining contemporary aesthetics and video technology – and reminiscent of old games – a multi-screen video installation takes Figaro as its subject.

The tour culminates in a multi-media homage to Mozart's opera *The Magic Flute*. Making use of mirrors, scenery, projections and light effects are combined in short versions of the opera from 1791 to the present. Film clips from legendary productions are inserted into the partly real and partly virtual scenery. A projected image of the public's timeless darling Papageno moves through time and space to present the most notable arias from *The Magic Flute*.

The decoration of Mozart's historic apartment on the first floor is intentionally different from the building's overall appearance so as to emphasize the distinctive nature and authenticity of the rooms.

## QUESTION MARK BY WAY OF INVITATION
### The reinstallation of Mozart's apartment
### on the first floor

A rethink of Mozart's apartment was called for when its function changed. For as long as this outstation of Wien Museum was restricted to the rooms in which the Mozart family lived, it had to offer as complete a picture of Mozart as possible in a compact space.

In the Mozarthaus, there are a further two floors available in which to tell the story of Vienna, Mozart and his music. The story line therefore had to be adapted and the contents condensed. The focus now lies exclusively on the highly productive years spent by Mozart in this fine apartment. How did he organize his work? What is known about the Mozarts' daily lives? How loud was it here? Where was the billiard table? Where did the servants sleep?

After making their way down through the house from the third floor to the first floor, visitors enter the Mozart apartment where they expect to encounter the spirit of the place. Yet what does a concept like "authenticity" really mean? What is fact, what fiction? Such questions were not to be avoided; instead they were to be addressed actively – and playfully. Atmosphere or information?; reconstruction or deconstruction?. Either option represents both an intellectual as well as a practical challenge for museum curators.

All too often in the past, musicians' homes were – and still are – called "memorials", a term suggestive of solemn and respectful commemoration of the dead, not unlike what is associated with a tomb of honor. Moreover, it was also the norm to bring the personal into play using ensembles of scenically arranged objects. To create atmosphere, ploys were resorted to: a rope placed in front of a bed or a cabinet-despite the fact that the furniture came from some antiques depot.

In the case of Mozart's Vienna apartment, the age of the historicizing cult of genius has long been a thing of the past. By 1995 at the latest, the redesign by the architect Elsa Prochazka resulted in radical minimization on which her skepticism towards the non-authentic left its mark. She took as her starting point the irreplaceability of the rooms. The apartment itself was thus defined as the "exhibit". On the one hand, her presentation was instructive and sparing; on the other hand, it included symbolic interventions intended to stress the "sensual level of hearing". One of the tasks for 2006 was to retain the high level of reflection prompted by the 1995 exhibit (and to leave in place all the poetically austere display units). At the same time, new connections between meanings were to be created, but above all, the public was to be invited to participate more and set off on the trail of Mozart.

More so than before, the tour is characterized by stories and information. They are conveyed not only through exhibits, but also through models, videos and a linguistic and spatial dialog with visitors. Questions marks, suppositions and speculation characterize this dialog – because controversy even surrounds how the rooms were used.

Is the "study" actually only a "study"? Hardly any items of furniture or objects that belonged to Mozart still exist. The two-and-a-half years the Mozarts lived in the building we now call the "Mozarthaus" were but a short interlude in its history.

Visitors must imagine for themselves what life here was once like, no differently than directors producing movies about Mozart. In the end, it is all down to the imagination. This – an open game with recognizable rules – is what guided the team of Werner Hanak (whose basic concept it is), Ulrike Spring and Wolfgang Kos, as well as the designer Kriso Leinfellner (Lichtwitz-Büro für visuelle Kommunikation/propeller z).

The rooms themselves are the authentic and original heart of the Mozart apartment: their order and propor- tions, what they look out on, diverse details. The empty shell, according to designer Kriso Leinfellner, had to be respected: "All the new elements such as lighting, equip- ment, pedestals and display units should not be confused with household articles and should have as little detail as possible." The materials are plain so as to avoid the creation of the inauthentic.

Selected pieces of furniture and items from Mozart's time are indeed present here and there, even if they were not his personal possessions. They have not been chosen arbitrarily; instead they are indicative of a room's prob- able uses at the time. The objects have been selected with reference to Mozart's estate.

As a musician's apartment presented in contemporary fashion pushes at the boundaries of presentation associat- ed with traditional museums, visitors should at least be given a few good questions to ask.

*"… I assure you that*
*this is a splendid place …"*

## VIENNA IN THE ERA OF MOZART

In Spring of 1781 Mozart arrived in one of Europe's most exciting capitals. Under the Emperor Joseph II Vienna had become a center of the Enlightenment and part of the political, intellectual and social renewal of the age. And at the heart of the city's cultural interests was music. It played a leading role not only at court or in the salons of the aristocracy, but in the homes of the prosperous middle class as well. Mozart was admired and supported by many aristocrats, but he was also welcome in intellectual circles and became an active Freemason. But this successful musical "star" with his enormous zest for life was also interested in the more earthly pleasures of Vienna: the coffee houses, fashions, balls, cards, gambling – and the beautiful women.

## MOZART DECIDES TO SETTLE IN VIENNA

*My dear father … I assure you that this is a splendid place –*
*and for my business the best city in the world.*
This is what Mozart wrote to his father in Salzburg on
April 4, 1781. He'd only arrived in Vienna a couple of days
before at the bidding of his employer, the Salzburg Prince-
Archbishop, Hieronymus Colloredo. The freedom-loving
composer was fed up with his position as badly-payed
court organist to Salzburg's ruling bishop. The legendary
kick in the pants with which Count Arco had expelled him
from the Viennese residence of the bishop was the excuse
Mozart had been waiting for and he gave up the position
in Salzburg.

When he arrived in Vienna he was 25 years old and
had spent almost twenty of those years traveling. He had
performed as a child prodigy throughout Europe, playing
for kings, emperors and in aristocratic salons. Already
as a teenager, his virtuoso piano playing and impressive
compositions had created a sensation. He was certain: In
the Imperial city of Vienna he would have a very bright
future indeed.

After two decades of travel, his life in Vienna was also
anything but settled. During the Viennese years he
changed his address thirteen times. Depending on how
many compositions had been commissioned or how much
money he had at the time, he lived either in great splendor
or in very modest quarters in the suburbs. The city map
of the exhibition gives an overview of Mozart's various
residences.

The Deutschordenshaus in the Singerstrasse 7 was at
that time the Viennese residence of the Salzburg Prince-
Archbishop Hieronymus Colleredo and it was here, in the
home of his employer, that Mozart lived from mid-March
to early May of 1781. This was also where they had their
final altercation on the 8th or 9th of May. With a quick

kick in the pants, Colloredo's chamberlain, Count Arco, propelled Mozart through the front gate and out of the bishop's employment.

Mozart's largest and most impressive domicile was in the Mozarthaus Vienna in the Schulerstrasse 8. Mozart lived here from September 29, 1784 to April 23, 1987. Among other things, it was here that he wrote the "Kleine Nacht-musik" and *Figaro*. This is why the Viennese refer to it as the "Figarohaus". Like many other homes of Mozart, the "Kleine Kayserhaus" in the Rauhensteingasse 8 has not been preserved. It was here that Mozart died while still working on his requiem.

The paintings in the exhibition show a selection of the houses, churches, theaters and squares which were important for Mozart's life in Vienna. The "Graben" for example, the so-called "navel of Vienna" which is busy day and night. Mozart lived twice midst in this favorite meeting place of the Viennese. St Stephan's Cathedral also played an important role in Mozart's life several times. There he married Constanze Weber and also applied for an unpaid position as musician. It was also here that his funeral took place.

Mozart spent his last ten years in a large city of great vitality. Under Joseph II Vienna was a center of the Enlightenment and its only equals were Paris and London. 50,000 people lived within the city walls and another 150,000 in the suburbs. Chronicles report that every day up to 3,500 coaches and 1,000 other vehicles were crammed together in the city's streets and squares. Unlike the sleepy little principality of Salzburg, music was being made everywhere, in the theaters and salons, the concert halls and the parks.

RUDOLF VON ALT/HURLIMANN
Panorama de Vienne publié par
Aataria & Co., n.d.
*Colored copper engraving, 99 x 31 cm*
*ÖNB Map collection*

When Mozart moved to Vienna in
1781, the center of town was still
surrounded by the medieval fortifica-
tions. Some 50,000 people lived
behind these bastions and the streets
were extremely crowded.

CARL SCHÜTZ
Michaelerplatz around 1783
*Ink drawing with water colors,*
*42.3 x 27.3 cm*
*Wien Museum*

The tract of the Hofburg facing the
old part of the city was at Michaelerplatz. Next to the imperial residence
was the court theatre. Mozart played
here several times as a soloist and
three of his operas had their Vienna
premieres here. These first performances were usually conducted by the
composer.

BERNARDO BELLOTTO
("CANALETTO")
Vienna Mehlmarkt 1759/60
*Oil on canvas, 155 x 116 cm*
*KHM*

The Mehlmarkt was the name of the
new market in the center of Vienna.
The dominating building was called
the "Mehlgrube". Mozart gave some
of his most important concerts here,
among them the six "Friday Concerts"
in February and March of 1785 when
the piano concerto in D minor (KV
466) was first performed. In this same
house lived Franz Sales von Greiner,
a royal councilor and Freemason. His
daughter, Karoline Pichler, tells in her

memoirs about the wonderful concerts that were put on for family
celebrations and how during Advent
and Lent there would be musicales
every Tuesday in their salon.

CARL SCHÜTZ
St. Stephan's seen from the north
with the Crucifix Chapel, 1792
*Colored copper engraving, 30.5 x 44.5 cm*
*Wien Museum*

The massive Cathedral of St. Stephan
played an important role in Mozart's
life several times, because, despite
his frequent moves, he almost always
remained within the cathedral parish.
It was here that he married Constanze.
He applied to the Vienna municipal
administration for an unpaid position
as cathedral musician. He was assured
of a position as conductor as soon as
one became vacant. The current conductor (Johann Leopold Hofmann)
was in failing health, but survived
nevertheless. And so the promise was
never kept. The composer's funeral
mass was celebrated here.

Letter of Employment naming
Mozart a court musician,
Vienna 1787
*Autograph, 29.3 x 44 cm*
*Salzburg ISM, Mozart Museum*

It took six years in Vienna before
Joseph II officially named the composer from Salzburg as a "Royal Court
Music Composer" and beginning on
December 7, 1787 he received 800
Gulden a year. Mozart's comment on
the not very generous salary was:
"It's too much for what I do and not
enough for what I could do." His
duties at court remained less than
challenging. A musical genius was
reduced to composing music for the
Emperor's masked balls. During the
four carnival seasons until 1791
Mozart composed 36 minuets and
at least 31 German dances.

CHECKPOINTMEDIA
Installation "Mozart's Residences
in Vienna"

## MOZART, THE DARLING OF VIENNESE SOCIETY

*I don't have to be an aristocrat to do what is right and just,*
*which is neither too much nor too little. It's our hearts that*
*confer nobility upon us and so, even though I'm not a count,*
*I still have more honor than many a count does.*
This is what Mozart assured his father in a letter from
Vienna of June 21, 1781. Father Leopold had been worried
about his son's morality and ability to succeed.

But the ambitious young artist discovered a wide range
of activities. Although it's true that as a result of
Joseph II's distaste for pomp and luxury the imperial court
had lost much of its importance as a center of social life,
there were still many lavish aristocratic households left:
twenty princes and seventy counts. All of them attached
great importance to letting the world see their own splendor. Their salons became the new centers for social and
intellectual life, for art and culture. One of the leading
institutions was the salon of the Countess Wilhelmina
Thun-Hohenstein. There, already in May of 1781, Mozart
played excerpts from his Munich opera success *Idomeneo*.

The portraits in the room show some of these prominent
aristocrats. Among them is the Russian ambassador in
Vienna, Dimitri Mikhailovitch Galitzin who was a supporter and patron of Mozart or the Countesses Marie Elisabeth, Marie Christine and Marie Karoline Thun-Hohenstein who were known as the "Three Graces" because of
their great beauty. Their house was one of the social and
intellectual centers of Vienna and Mozart visited frequently. He admired them for their enlightened way of thinking.

Mozart soon got to know the intellectual elite of Vienna.
Here there are for example portraits of the scholar and
director of the Court Library Joseph von Sonnenfels, the
educational reformer Baron Gottfried van Swieten and the
director of the court theater Franz Xaver Wolfgang Count
of Orsini-Rosenberg. In addition to these illustrious per-

sonalities, Mozart also got to know such unusual and imposing figures as the "Court Moor" Angelo Soliman, an educator and gentleman scholar who was in the service of the princes of Liechtenstein.

As the new favorite of the Vienna audiences, Mozart enchanted ever larger circles of the city's society with a fireworks of musical events. Nobles of every rank, scientists, merchants and manufacturers streamed into the concert halls for Mozart's "Academies", the concerts which he organized and financed himself. The subscription list for a concert series in the Trattner-Hof in 1784 has been preserved. It has 176 names.

The excitement over Mozart only died down in later years. Austria was at war and the Emperor was leading his troops against the Turks. Money was scarce, a war tax was levied and there was a sense of crisis. Several times there were hunger riots. But through his aristocratic contacts Mozart had also gained access to intellectual circles. He got to know men who were passionately in favor of the Enlightenment and became acquainted with a whole new world of ideas: the idea of a republic, of universal human rights, tolerance and emancipation as well as educational, economic and social reforms. With his naturally acute mind, Mozart soon acquired a new education in this intellectual milieu, an education that was to inspire his music as well, right down to his last opera, *The Magic Flute*.

ANTON GRAFF
Joseph Edler von Sonnenfels,
before 1779
*Oil on canvas, 44.5 x 63 cm*
*Archive of the University of Vienna*

Joseph von Sonnenfels (1732–1817)
was not only a political and legal
theorist and one of the most important strategists of Joseph II's reform
policies, he also took an active part
in legal reform. As professor at the
University of Vienna, privy councilor
at court and president of the Academy
of Art he did his best to support a
number of causes: the abolition of
judicial torture, preventing pirated
editions of books and getting clowns
off the stage. Sonnenfels was also
founder of the *Freemason's Journal*
and was a prominent member of the
same lodge as Mozart.

VICTOR CLAVEREAU
Gottfried Freiherr van Swieten, n.d.
*Pastel, 47.5 x 58 cm*
*Wien Museum*

Gottfried Freiherr van Swieten
(1734–1803) was the son of the
Empress Maria Theresia's personal
physician, an educational reformer
and director of the Court Library.
He was one of the leading members
of the circle promoting Joseph II's
reforms. Beginning in 1786 he founded a society of "Associated Cavaliers".
This group organized performances
of oratorios, first under the conductor Joseph Starzer and then under
Mozart. Van Swieten had been Austrian ambassador in Prussia where he
became acquainted with Carl Philipp
Emanuel Bach. It was one of his great
ambitions to familiarize the music-
lovers of Vienna with the work of
Johann Sebastian Bach. He may well
have been an eye-witness to Mozart's
death and he both paid for and organized Mozart's funeral. Afterwards, he
temporarily took Constanze into his
home and cared for Mozart's eldest
son.

JOHANN GOTTFRIED HAID
Portrait of Angelo Soliman, n.d.
*Copper engraving, 32.4 x 45.3 cm*
*Wien Museum*

Known as the "princely Moor" The
African chieftan's son, Angelo Soliman
was a personage with an imposing
presence. He was part of Mozart's
circle and served the princes of
Liechtenstein both as first valet as
well as tutor for the prince's son.
The protocols of the Masonic lodge
"True Harmony" show that this is
where he and Mozart met. Angelo
Soliman had been captured as a child
and was brought to Marseille where
he was taken into service of a Sicilian
Marquise in Messina. She gave him
as a gift to Prince Lobkowitz, who at
that time was the Imperial Governor
of Sicily. After the death of the prince
he became part of the Liechtenstein
household. Angelo Soliman's body
was mummified and was exhibited in
a  royal cabinet of "natural curiosi-
ties". When this royal cabinet was
burned during the revolution of 1848,
his body was lost as well.

FRIEDRICH HEINRICH FÜGER
The Countesses Thun-Hohenstein,
around 1788
*Oil on canvas, 40 x 53 cm*
*Österreichische Galerie*

Because of their great beauty, the
Countesses Marie Elisabeth, Marie
Karoline and Marie Christine Thun-
Hohenstein were known in Vienna
as the "Three Graces". Their house
was one of the intellectual and social
centers of Vienna. They showed themselves to be both patronesses as well
as gifted amateur musicians. Mozart
visited their house frequently and
thought highly of them because of
their enlightened attitudes. In 1789
Mozart traveled to Berlin with Marie
Christine's husband, Prince Lichnowsky and both men were Freemasons.

## WORLD EVENTS IN THE AGE OF MOZART

A selection of the most important historical events shows that Mozart lived in a time of transition and that it was reflected in his work.

Joseph II with his Two Sisters

The American Declaration of Independence (1776)

**1740–80** Reign of Maria Theresia (1717–1780) in Austria, Bohemia and Hungary.

**1745–65** Franz I Stephan of Lothringen (1708–1765), consort of Maria Theresia, rules as Holy Roman Emperor.

**1753–71** Sigmund Christoph Count of Schrattenbach (1698–1771) rules as Prince-Archbishop of Salzburg.

**1756** Under Louis XV (1710–1774) France becomes an ally of Austria.

**1756–63** The Seven Years War in Europe; the French and Indian War in North America. George III (1738–1820) is King of England.

**1761** Joseph Haydn (1732–1809) enters the service of Prince Ester-házy.

**1765–90** Joseph II (1741–1790), the oldest son of Maria Theresia becomes Holy Roman Emperor on the death of his father in 1765. He is co-regent of the patrimonial lands together with his mother until her death in 1780.

**1770** On May 16th Louis XVI (1754–1793) of France marries Marie-Antoinette of Austria.

**1770–90** Inspired by Joseph II's ideas, a number of purpose-built buildings are constructed in Vienna, such as the Starhemberg house and the General Hospital.

**1772–1803** Hieronymus Joseph Franz de Paula Count Colloredo (1732–1812) is Prince-Archbishop of Salzburg.

**1773** The Jesuit order is dissolved by Pope Clement XIV (1705–1774). On August 5th the Mozarts are received in audience by Empress Maria Theresia.

**1775–83** American War of Independence.

**1776** Through an initiative of Joseph Sonnenfels (1773–1817) judicial torture is abolished in Austria.
American Declaration of Independence.

**1780–90** As successor to Maria Theresia, Joseph II carries out many reforms in the Austrian patrimonial lands (the abolition of serfdom; closure of numerous monasteries; religious freedom, church reform; introduction of civil marriage; permission for non-Catholics to immigrate to Austria, etc.).

Friedrich Schiller, *The Robbers,* first performed 1782

The Marquis de Sade

Joseph II at War Against the Turks

Casanova's Flight from the Lead
Chambers of Vienna

Adolph Freiherr von Knigge,
*On Dealing with Other People*, 1788

**1781** June 4: Alliance between
Austria and Russia.

**1782** Pope Pius VI (1717–1799)
visits Munich and Vienna.
Schiller's play *The Robbers* is first
performed in Mannheim.
The last European witch-burning in
Glarus (Switzerland).

**1783** Peace of Versailles: England
recognizes the independence of the
USA.

**1784** 26 April: Performance of
Pierre-Augustin Caron de Beau-
marchais' (1732–1799) comedy
*La folle Journée ou Le Mariage de
Figaro* in Paris.
De Sade: *The 120 Days of Sodom.*

**1786–97** Friedrich Wilhelm II
(1744–1797) is King of Prussia.
Gottfried August Bürger: *Münch-
hausen.*
First steam ship (on the Delaware).
First ascent of Mont Blanc.

**1787** November 15: Christoph
Willibald Gluck dies in Vienna.
United States Constitution.
A new Austrian code of law that
forbids torture.

**1787–92** Together with Russia,
Austria fights it last war against
the Turks.

**1788** Casanova: *The History of
my Flight from the Lead Chambers.*
Knigge: *On Dealing with other
People, a Handbook of Manners.*

**1789** Beginning of the French Revolution. August 26: Proclamation of the Rights of Man.

**1789–97** George Washington (1732–1799) first President of the United States.

**1790** Death of Joseph II, succeeded by Leopold II.
Goethe: First version of *Faust*.

Eugène Delacroix, *Freedom Leading the People*, 1830

**1790–92** Leopold II (1747–1792) repeals some of the reforms of Joseph II.

**1791** First constitution of the French Revolution: France becomes a constitutional monarchy.
Luigi Galvani: *On the Electrical Powers of Muscle Movements*.
Birth of the Austrian writer Franz Grillparzer in Vienna.
Joseph Haydn composes his Symphony in C Major (the "Surprize Symphony").

Johann Heinrich Wilhelm Tischbein, *Goethe in the Campagna*, 1786/87

The Death of Emperor Joseph II on February 20, 1790

*Concluserunt multitudinem copiosam... llem... prent une grande quantité...*
*Dirumpebatur autem rete eorum... et ait:... et leur filet rompoit... mais il n'étne craignne point;*
*noli timere; ex hoc jam homines eris capiens.... votre emploi d'énormais sera, de prendre des hommes....*

*Sie fingen eine grosse Menge... und ihr Netz zerriss... aber Cyrisch... fürchte Dich nicht; von nun an wirst du Menschen fischen....*

## C. J. METTENLEITER AFTER MANSFELD

*The Triumph of the Liberal Ideas of Joseph II, n. d.*
*Copper engraving, 43 x 58.5 cm*
*Wien Museum*

An allegory doing homage to the liberal reform policies of Joseph II. His idea was to use tolerance and enlightenment for the welfare of the state. For example: The Emperor issued edicts of religious toleration for Greek Orthodox Christians, Jews and Protestants. At the same time he made inroads into the rights of the Catholic church through the closure of 400 Austrian monasteries and a reform of both the liturgy and burial customs. His reforms created strong resistance on the part of the church but he was supported and encouraged by the intellectual elite around Mozart.

## MOZART AND THE FREEMASONS

After the overture to *Don Giovanni* has faded away, we hear Leporello sing: "Non voglio piu servir": He no longer wants to serve; he no longer wants a master telling him what to do. Mozart was in much the same mood when he fled from Salzburg to Vienna. He intended to leave the service of the Prince-Archbishop Colloredo and escape from the domination of his father, Leopold. Vienna was imperial capital and a center of culture.

Solely on the basis of his boundless talent alone (he is, after all, 'World Genius Number One') Mozart would certainly have been a success in Vienna. His membership in the Freemasons did, however, help him to become well-known in Viennese society a bit faster.

Since the beginning of the century, the English philosopher John Locke, and the Scot David Hume, together with French scholars, authors and literati such as Diderot and d'Alembert (the so-called "Encyclopédistes") had changed the intellectual climate in Europe. A thousand years of feudal class structure began to crumble. The social and economic order began to develop chaotic elements. The Enlightenment tried to reorder the world on the basis of reason and the times were ripe for a revolution. "I no longer want to serve" was the secret credo of the progressive sections of the population.

Mozart was something of a rebel even before he came to Vienna and his revolutionary spirit was open to the new ideals of freedom. In Vienna he encountered the people he had been hoping for. The intellectual elite of the capital, large sections of the nobility, government officials, scholars, writers and musicians were joined together in the Masonic lodges and determined to support the enlightened (but despotic) policies of Joseph II. At the meetings of the lodge, social barriers were disregarded. Here, men of good reputation could meet with each other as equals and form cells of democratic thought under an absolutist regime.

A fresh impetus was at hand and the Emperor promulgated one reform after the other. And although he put strict limits on the number of lodges allowed, he also issued an edict giving the Freemasons legal status.

Mozart was an enthusiastic and fervent Mason who enjoyed the affection and respect of his fellow members. We know that he performed music in the various lodges and thereby contributed to the solemn atmosphere of the meetings. Many of the songs he composed were intended for use in the lodge. He composed the Masonic Funeral Music for two noblemen. What's more, in the last weeks before his death he stopped working on the *Requiem* and didn't complete the "Dies Irae". Instead he wrote the Masonic song "Ode to Friendship" (KV 625).

The meaning and spirit of freemasonry became the crowning achievement of his life. It completed his personality and had an influence on his magnificent compositions which isn't fully appreciated even today.

On December 14, 1784, together with chaplain Wenzel Summer, Mozart was inducted into a lodge named "Benevolence". After the apprentice and journeyman phases, he became a master Mason. There are very few documents in Mozart's hand relating to Freemasonry. In one letter to his father he refers to their both being members. In the visitors' book of a friend he wrote a dedication in English. Visits to the Viennese lodges were carefully noted down. One indication of how important Freemasonry was to him is that he encouraged both his father Leopold and his teacher Joseph Haydn to join.

After his death Mozart's body was laid out in a chapel above the entrance to the catacombs of St. Stephan's. The funeral mass was also celebrated there. A few days afterward, a solemn funeral ceremony took place in his lodge. The funeral oration has been preserved.

His opera *The Magic Flute*, however, remains an eternal testimony to the intimate connection between Mozart and the Freemasons. In the figure of Sarastro, Mozart gave us a portrait of one of the most important Freemasons of his time: the royal councillor for coinage and mining Ignaz von Born. He was the master who had promoted Mozart to journeyman.

Freemason
*Wiener Porzellanmanufaktur, ca. 1755*
*Porcelain, Height 14.5 cm*

This figurine shows the ideal image
of an 18th century Freemason. Next to
him is a stone which will be fitted
together with others to create a
building with human dimensions,
a "Temple of Solomon".

Page from a Book by
Joseph Bauernjöpel
*Facsimile, Vienna, 1793*
*17 x 21 cm*

This collection by Joseph Bauernjöpel
is much like a collage with copper
engravings pasted in and other illus-
trations. The introduction deals with
the origins of Freemasonry, the "harmony of creation" and the "teachings
of nature". This is followed by four
sections describing the Masonic rituals and symbols customary in the Austrian Empire during the last third of
the 18th century. He describes the
admission of apprentices, journeymen
and masters as well as other cere-
monies and also provides a clear and
precise overview of the work of the
lodges during this period. Mozart
doubtless knew about these rituals
and they gave him ideas for the initia-
tions of Pamina and Tamino in *The
Magic Flute.*

### Freemason's Sash

*Petersham wool, metal threads, metal sequins, glass stones*
*Austria, last quarter of the*
*18th century*
*55.5 x 43.5 cm*

The sash used a wide variety of important Masonic symbols such as the "Flaming Star" (above) and, below that, of the construction of the temple. In addition, there are other symbols more directly related to construction work: a plumb bob, a trowel, a hammer, a compass and an angular measure.

### A Freemason "Bijou"

*Silver-plated metal, glass stones*
*Austria, last fourth of the 18th century*
*7.1 x 4.5 cm*

This badge was known as a "Bijou" and indicated particular degrees of membership and lodges. They were intended to convey a maximum of information in a very small space. This 18th century bijou uses the old allegory of the pelican. She tears open her own breast to feed her young with her own blood. This expressed the themes of brotherly love, self-sacrifice and other Christian virtues.

### Freemason's Apron

*Silk, metal threads, metal plates and metal sequins, gilded, embroidery*
*Austria, last fourth of the 18th century*
*29 x 32 cm*

The compass and angular measure of the apron point to the profession of mason and the two columns refer to the Temple of Solomon. By putting on such an apron a Freemason showed himself to be working on a great "construction project" – the temple of universal humanitarianism. In other words, the work of the Freemason should encourage their members to treat others more humanely.

## THE TURBULENT LIFE OF
## WOLFGANG AMADEUS MOZART

*I want to have everything that is good and genuine and beautiful.* This is the personal credo that Mozart expressed in a letter to his close friend Baroness Elisabeth Waldstätten, a person he revered deeply.

Mozart was hungry for life and firmly determined to enjoy to the fullest all the fashionable luxury and excitement a great metropolis has to offer. He visited coffee houses, played cards, billiards and gambled illegally. For a time he kept his own coach and horse and spent money on expensive books. And when it came to clothing, he gave Baroness Waldstätten a rather broad hint in a letter: *And as far as that beautiful red coat is concerned, I'm afraid it's eating away cruelly at my innermost heart. I beg of you, tell me where I might get it and how much it costs. Because I simply must have a coat like that, if only because then it would be worthwhile to have the buttons put on it – the ones I've been dreaming of for ever so long. They're mother of pearl with some sort of white stones along the side and a beautiful yellow stone in the middle.*

The baroness took the hint and he got that coat he just couldn't live without. Reproductions show the fashionable men's clothing of Mozart's period.

Baroness Waldstätten also proved useful in helping to overcome Mozart's father's long and stubborn resistance to the marriage with Constanze. But despite the difficult beginnings, their marriage proved a happy one. During the nine years they were together they had six children, but only two survived to adulthood.

In Mozart's house there was almost always a jolly atmosphere, visitors came and went and friends, musicians and students were always made to feel welcome. Punch in particular seems to have been consumed in considerable quantities. But this opulent life style also used up incredible sums of money. More than twenty times Mozart was forced to write imploring letters, begging for money from his generous friend and supporter the textile manufacturer Johann Michael Puchberg.

Over four years Puchberg loaned Mozart a total of 1,515 Gulden. During this time Mozart was earning fees appropriate to the star that he was – a cautious estimate would be 9,150 Gulden. These are gigantic sums of money compared with what it cost a normal, middle class family to live a decent life. Contemporary sources indicate that 1,000 Gulden was considered a comfortable yearly income. Even Mozart's extravagances don't quite explain where all the money went.

Modern Mozart researchers have been able to disprove the old cliché that he died in abject poverty. Today, they suspect that Mozart had been attending secret gambling sessions where huge sums were being bet. Gambling debts were debts of honor and had to be repaid immediately. Because the gambling was illegal, such debts were never written down. It was only in 1992 that a handwritten note of Mozart's came to light. It's dated between 1786 and 1788. Here, the composer presumably noted down his winnings and losses at the gambling table. Mozart researchers tend to interpret this note as indicating an income of 6,843 Gulden and 14 Kreuzer (in various currencies). But his expenses were such that he ended up with a deficit of 4,377 Gulden and 34 Kreuzer which had to be divided up among five creditors.

JOSEPH LANGE
Portrait of Constanze Mozart, n.d.
*Oil on canvas, 24.8 x 32.3 cm*
*Glasgow, Hunterian Museum*

The actor and painter Joseph Lange
portrayed Constanze Mozart
(1762–1842) during the early years of
her marriage. Lange had been married
since 1780 to Constanze's sister
Aloysia Weber. Mozart married Constanze against the will of her father.
Of the six children they had together
only two sons survived: Carl Thomas
(1784–1858) and Franz Xaver
Wolfgang (1791–1844). Both sons
remained unmarried. After his death,
Constanze took an active role in
administering his estate. The role she
played in this connection has been
controversial. Her second husband,
the Dane Georg Nikolaus Nissen
(1776–1826) wrote the first Mozart
biography under her direction.

JOHANN PEZZL
*Faustin*, Zürich 1783
*Mozarthaus Vienna*

The writer and government official
Johann Pezzl (1756–1823) published
his Enlightenment novel *Faustin* for
the first time in Zürich in 1783. Pezzl
was librarian to Prince Kaunitz and
frequented Enlightenment circles in
Vienna. From 1785 on he was a member of the Lodge 'Palm Tree' and in
1791 he became an official of the
Lodge.

### HIERONYMUS LÖSCHENKOHL
Musical Deck of Cards, Vienna 1806,
52 cards
*Colored copper engravings,*
*6.7 x 10.1 cm*
*Wien Museum*

The etcher and engraver Löschenkohl
not only made silhouettes and drew
landscapes, he also produced greeting
cards and playing cards. The Mozart
family loved card games and played
frequently. They also played using
French playing cards with musical
motifs – including motifs from
Mozart's own compositions.

### PATER HILARION
"Dance Halls" from *Gallery of*
*Worldly Abuses*, Frankfurt 1785
(selection)
*Copper engraving, max. 9.55 x 16.28 cm;*
*min. 8.2 x 12.8 cm*
*WStLB*

As an active member of Viennese
society, Mozart loved attending the
carnival or Mardi Gras celebrations
and balls. In a letter to his father
Leopold he asked that a costume be
sent to him from Salzburg. As court
composer he wrote primarily dance
music for the masked balls in the
Imperial Palace.
This series of copper engravings is
taken from the *Gallery of Worldly*
*Abuses* by Pater Hilarion. In this book
he made fun of the social excesses of
his own time and urged more rational
behavior.

**CARL SCHÜTZ**
On the "Graben" with a view
to the Kohlmarkt, 1782
*Colored copper engraving and etching,*
*42,5 x 32,9 cm*
*Wien Museum*

**CHECKPOINTMEDIA**
"The Nymphs of the Graben"

This installation shows the "Graben".
It is not far from St. Stephan's Cathedral and was a center of social life. In
the evenings, elegant young men came
here to meet up with the "Nymphs of
the Graben", young women whose
love could be had for a price.

*"… your son is
the greatest composer …"*

## MOZART'S MUSICAL WORLD

Mozart's arrival in Vienna coincided with an attempt by the Emperor Joseph II to reduce the splendor of the Imperial court. This also meant less money being spent on music. But the almost one hundred families who made up the city's higher nobility did not want to dispense with the luxury they had grown used to. Together with the rising middle class, they made sure that Vienna continued to attract singers, musicians, conductors and composers like a magnet. Mozart had a lot of competition to deal with. His most important rival was the Italian composer Antonio Salieri. But at the same time, Mozart also found friends and supporters, such as Joseph Haydn. It was in Vienna, during the last ten years of his life that Mozart composed his greatest works.
His fame as an opera composer is based on *The Marriage of Figaro*, which, like his next two works, *Don Giovanni* and *Così fan tutte*, was written in collaboration with the librettist Lorenzo da Ponte. Together with the delightful *The Magic Flute* and his *Requiem* they are part of a musical heritage that will live forever.

## WOLFGANG AMADEUS MOZART
## AND VIENNA, THE CITY OF MUSIC

*Herr Haydn told me: I swear to you before God and as an honest man that your son is the greatest composer I have ever known in person or by name. He has taste and beyond that the most enormous skill and artistry.*

Already during his own lifetime Joseph Haydn was one of the most famous composers of the Habsburg Empire. And so, it's not surprising that Mozart's father Leopold immediately wrote a letter to his daughter Nannerl in Salzburg to tell her the good news.

In 1785 Leopold Mozart arrived in Vienna to visit his son for a few months. Mozart and his young wife had just moved into a large and elegant apartment in the Schulerstrasse and so there was plenty of space for Leopold. A private concert was arranged to welcome his father. The guest of honor was Joseph Haydn who at that time was in the service of Prince Esterházy. Together with the Barons Anton and Bartholomäus Tinti, Mozart father and son played three new string quartets. Later, Mozart added three others and dedicated all six of them to his revered friend Joseph Haydn.

Vienna was a music center that acted like a magnet for singers, musicians, soloists and ensembles as well as for composers and conductors. All of them were trying to become famous and Mozart had a great deal of competition. But he also found friends such as the concertmaster of the court theater, Paul Wranitzky. He too was one of Mozart's fellow masons. In addition to Haydn, Mozart was also supported by the Neapolitan composer Giuseppe Bonno. A court composer and conductor, Bonno introduced Mozart to Viennese music-lovers with a concert in 1781. It included one of Mozart's symphonies and showed what this young composer could do.

At that time the controversial ruler of the Viennese musical scene was the composer Christoph Willibald Gluck. He was a musical patriarch. His career began long before Mozart was born and at the Imperial court his views dominated the opera repertoire. Gluck had become prominent as a reformer of opera and wanted to transcend the rigid conventions of Italian and French opera. He wanted serious works with genuine expression and truthfulness.

But there was another composer at court who exercised considerable influence. Antonio Salieri was a specialist for the much-loved Italian operas. He had lived in Vienna since 1766 and had been named a court conductor. One of his most popular successes was *Axur, re d'Ormus*. Only once, during the carneval of 1786 were Mozart and Salieri ever in direct competition. At a celebration in the palace orangerie that Joseph II gave in honor of his sister Maria Christina, the Italian opera and the German-language "Singspiel" met head on. Salieri's *Prima la musica, poi le parole* was in competition with Mozart's *Schauspieldirektor*. The taste of the aristocratic guests favored the opera buffa. Salieri received 100 Gulden, Mozart only half that.

Posterity has magnified this competition between Mozart and Salieri into an embittered hostility. It's even been suggested that Salieri poisoned his rival out of hatred and envy. In January of 1824, Beethoven noted in his journal that, "Salieri is falling apart. He has fantasies that he was responsible for Mozart's death and that he gave him poison." No proof has ever been found that Mozart was poisoned. The animosity they felt was certainly mutual. Mozart's first biographer was Constanze's second husband Nissen. He reports that Mozart could sit down at the piano and give brilliant off-the cuff parodies of "a certain Italian composer."

ANTON GRASSI
Joseph Haydn, 1799
*Bust, bisquit porcellan, cast,*
*height 40 cm*
*Wien Museum*

The composer Joseph Haydn
(1732–1809) belonged to the musical
elite of his time. In 1761 he went into
the service of Prince Esterházy in
Eisenstadt. There he remained until
the death of Prince Nicolas Joseph
in 1790. Afterwards, he worked in
Vienna, made two trips to England
and was honored throughout Europe.
Ludwig van Beethoven was one of
his pupils. Haydn wrote symphonies,
operas, masses, sonatas and string
quartets. He was a frequent guest in
Mozart's home. The letters of Leopold
Mozart show what a high opinion he
had of his young friend.

ANONYMOUS
Portrait of Paul Wranitzky, n.d.
*Oil on canvas, 44 x 56 cm*
*Collections of the Gesellschaft der*
*Musikfreunde*

A portrait of the Bohemian musician
Paul Wranitzky (1756–1808). He was
a musical director, concertmaster to
Count Johann Nepomuk Esterházy,
concertmaster of the Royal Theater
and both a good friend of Mozart as
well as a fellow Freemason.

ANONYMOUS
Portrait of Muzio Clementi, n.d.
*Oil on canvas, 44 x 56 cm*
*Collections of the Gesellschaft der*
*Musikfreunde*

Portrait of the Italian pianist and composer Muzio Clementi (1752–1832).
During a concert tour in Vienna he
performed before Emperor Joseph II
on Christmas Eve and played in competition with Mozart. The Emperor
gave them a theme upon which both
of them had to improvise.

JEAN SIFFRED DUPLESSIS
Portrait of Christoph Willibald
Gluck, ca. 1775
*Oil on canvas, 99.5 x 80.05 cm*
*KHM*

After studying in Italy and England
Christoph W. Gluck (1714–1787) came
to Vienna in 1750 and after 1754
worked at the Hofburg Theater.
Already during his own lifetime he
was considered the best and most
important musician of the period. He
was also an important opera reformer.
In *Orfeo ed Euridice, Alceste* and the
two *Iphigenie* operas he tried to overcome the rigid conceptions which had
dominated opera up until that time.
His goal was to put the music in the
service of the text and make the
course of the action more fluid. Even
so, most of Glucks 47 operas remained
dominated by traditional forms. After
Glucks death, Mozart was named
chamber musican at court. Mozart,
however, was paid only 800 Gulden
instead of the 2,000 which Gluck had
received.

JOSEPH WILLIBROD MÄHLER
Portrait of Antonio Salieri, n.d.
*Oil on canvas, 44 x 56 cm*
*Collections of the Gesellschaft der*
*Musikfreunde*

The Italian composer Antonio Salieri
(1750–1825) was one of Mozart's main
competitors. He succeeded Giuseppe
Bonno as court composer after he had
already made a name for himself as a
composer of operas and church music.
Salieri wrote some of the most inter-
nationally successful operas of his
time. After the death of Joseph II, he
lost his positions at court and became
a music teacher. Constanze Mozart
entrusted the musical education of
her son to him.

ANONYMOUS
Portrait of Giuseppe Bonno, n.d.
*Oil on canvas, 44 x 56 cm*
*Collections of the Gesellschaft der*
*Musikfreunde*

Portrait of the Neapolitan composer
Giuseppe Bonno (1711–1788).

## THE MARRIAGE OF FIGARO

*In our day anything that's forbidden to say gets sung.*
This was the commentary of the newspaper *Wiener Realzeitung* on July 11, 1786 after the premiere of the "Comedia per musica" *The Marriage of Figaro (Le nozze di Figaro)* at the National-Court Theater.

Mozart wrote his famous comic opera in the house at Schulerstrass 8. The Viennese still call it the "Figaro House". It was based on a work of literature that was as famous as it was infamous: the revolutionary comedy *La folle Journée ou Le Mariage de Figaro* by Pierre-Augustin Caron de Beaumarchais. The play had had a triumphal premiere at the Comédie Française in 1784 two years before Mozart's opera was first performed. It had taken the play six years to get through the French censors.

Biting and brilliant at the same time, Beaumarchais makes fun of the mores of an aristocratic society and even questions the authority of the aristocracy itself. Only a year after the premiere in Paris, this social satire was to have been performed in Vienna on the stage of the Kärntnertor-Theater. At the last minute the Emperor personally intervened and prevented the performance.

We don't know exactly when Mozart first got to read Beaumarchais' work. What is sure, however, is that Lorenzo da Ponte was the one who suggested the play as the basis for an opera. According to da Ponte's memoirs it took all his powers of persuasion to coax the Emperor into giving his permission. Da Ponte changed the stage play in a very clever way. He softened much of the explosive satire and emphasized the battle between the sexes.

A successful rebellion of servants against their masters' aristocratic misuse of power was something completely new in the history of comic opera. It showed the victory of an "aristocracy of the heart" over the aristocracy of privilege. But what was equally new was the incomparable musical mixture of wistfulness and wit, of rebellion and passion.

*Figaro* is Mozart's most political opera. Many of Vienna's aristocrats didn't like it one bit and it cost him a lot of sympathy in certain quarters. But the Emperor had given his permission and even attended the general rehearsal. Mozart's hopes for a triumphal success at the premiere on May 1, 1786 were, however, not to be fulfilled. One newspaper reported that attempts were made to disturb the performance: "hot-headed young fellows in the upper balconies screamed their well-paid lungs out." The newspaper also reported, however, that, "The music of Herr Mozart is an artistic masterpiece." Even so, the opera was taken out of the repertoire after only nine other performances that year.

But only half a year after the premiere in Vienna, the music-loving city of Prague was gripped in a "Figaro Fever". Adoring poems about Mozart were printed and distributed in the streets. Mozart wrote his friend Gottfried von Jacquin about the enthusiastic reception his opera had had: *I was pleased as punch to see the way all these people took the music from my Figaro, transformed it into quadrilles and German dances and then hopped about for all it was worth. Because here, people speak of nothing except Figaro. Nothing gets played, or blown, or sung, or whistled – except Figaro. No one goes to any opera – except Figaro and yet again Figaro. It's a great honor for me.*

This social portrait that shows feminine cunning triumphing over male desire plays in part in the idyllic surroundings of an aristocratic garden idyll. Parks and gardens were popular with both nobles and commoners alike. As an enlightened monarch, Joseph II opened the Augarten, the Prater and the royal hunting preserve to the whole populace so that they could take a refreshing walk or just go there for the fun of it. Mozart also liked the Prater and it is thought that he kept a horse there. But Mozart also knew and loved the green refuges of the Viennese aristocracy. The Enlightenment inspired the noble landowners from Mozart's circle of friends to a change of attitude. They abandoned the formal splendor of the old baroque gardens and now preferred more natural, romantic landscapes.

HIERONYMUS LÖSCHENKOHL
The New Joy in the Prater
*Etching washed over with brush
and Indian ink, 69.50 x 50 cm
(oval 63.6 x 47.1 cm)
Albertina*

Emperor Joseph II decided that the
entire population should be able to
share in the beauty and joys of well-
tended gardens and parks. And so
this enlightened monarch opened the
Prater, a royal hunting preserve, as a
place for all the Viennese to prome-
nade. The garden views shown in the
exhibition are intended as a background to the action of *The Marriage
of Figaro.*

Program for the Premiere of
*The Marriage of Figaro*, 1786
*Print, 41.5 x 33 cm
ÖNB, Theatersammlung (Theatermuseum)*

The premiere of *The Marriage of
Figaro* was on May 1, 1786 in the
National-Court Theater. It was based
on Beaumarchais' scandalous comedy
*La folle Journée ou le Mariage de Figaro.*

HIERONYMUS LÖSCHENKOHL
Francesco Benucci,
the first Figaro, n.d.
*Silhouette from the "Wiener Musik-
und Theater-Almanach"
Print, 5 x 8 cm
WStLB*

Together, the silhouettes form a group
portrait of the most important singers
of the premiere. Figaro was sung by
Francesco Benucci, a bass and buffo
who Mozart admired greatly. Cherubi-
no was sung by Dorothea Bussani from
Vienna. It was her musical debut
and she was married to the Bartolo,
the Italian singer Francesco Bussani.
The Irish tenor buffo Michael O'Kelly
appeared as Don Basilio and he too
was a good friend of Mozart. The
roles of Marcelina and Count Almavi-
va were sung by the married couple
Maria and Stefano Mandini who had
both been hired in Vienna in 1783.
The acclaimed Italian soprano Luisa
Laschi-Mombelli was the first Countess. Susanna was sung by the English
soprano Nancy Storace, a primadonna
with a great comic talent. When she
left Vienna in 1787, he wrote the concert aria "Non temer amato bene" for
her.

Historical Murals

Mozart's apartment in the "Figaro House" was described by his father as being "quite a pretty place with all the embellishments such a house should have." And indeed, the rooms on all floors were decorated with an opulence usually found only in aristocratic homes. There was ornamental plasterwork on the ceilings and the walls were covered with painted murals. The exposed sections of the murals give an impression of their quality.

Restorers have discovered more than 40 layers of paint that have been applied to these walls over the past 250 years. The exposed section shows how the walls were structured into frames and panels as "painted stone". This layer is on top of 12 other layers (some of which remain only as fragments) and is particularly well preserved. Although it was painted in the early 19th century, it took over a wall decoration system that had existed before and during Mozart's time. Not all panels were painted to imitate stone, and, instead, some were decorated with painted silk wall-hangings with floral or striped patterns.

CHECKPOINTMEDIA
Installation "Figaro over the Centuries"

A video dice game using Figaro portrayals of the past two hundred years

## COSÌ FAN TUTTE

*I think you'll like the arietta I wrote for Ferrarese.*
Letter of Mozart to Constanze in August, 1789.

La Ferrarese's real name was Adriana Gabrieli and she was one of the Italian primadonnas at the National Court Theater. At the first performance of Mozart's opera buffa *Così fan tutte* she sang the Fiordiligi. Both Mozart and his librettist Lorenzo da Ponte admired her a great deal. In his memoirs, *My Adventurous Life* he wrote of her, "… her voice was divine, her singing methods quite new and unusually appealing.

Mozart had been working on this comedy of mistaken identities since the summer of 1789. The subtitle, The *School for Lovers* was a reference to a successful work by Mozart's rival Antonio Salieri, *The School of the Jealous*. The plot of the play possibly alludes to an instance of partner swapping in Viennese high society. The idea of using a piece of gossip that even the police had followed up as the material for an opera supposedly came from the Emperor Joseph II himself. His National Court Theater commissioned Mozart to write a comic opera for the carneval season of 1789/90.

*Così fan tutte* had its premiere on January 26, 1790 as the last piece of the current season. It had a brilliant cast including not only La Ferrarese but such stars as Dorothea Bussani or Francesco Benucci who sang Guglielmo. Mozart admired Benucci greatly and he had been the first Figaro. But the audience wasn't quite so enthusiastic about this bit of theatrical fun. The references to persons and situations in the city were a bit too obvious. The Emperor couldn't attend the premiere because he had contracted tuberculosis and was close to death. And so when the Emperor died on February 20, 1790 the run of performances had to be broken off after only five performances and the theater remained closed until April 11th. Between then and the end of August it was performed five more times and then vanished from the repertory. Only in 1794, three years after Mozart's death, did Emanuel Schikaneder bring out a new production.

## DON GIOVANNI

In his memoirs, Lorenzo da Ponte described his work on the libretto for *Don Giovanni:* "At night I write for Mozart and all the time I'm thinking about *Dante's* Inferno."

After Mozart's triumph with *Figaro* at the Nostitz Theater, Prague gave him a commission to write another opera. Pasquale Bondini, the impresario of the Prague opera house asked him to write an opera as part of the festivities to celebrate the upcoming visit of Prince Anton Clemens of Saxony and his bride Archduchess Maria Theresia of Austria. Because of their good history of collaboration, Mozart once again chose da Ponte as his librettist. Da Ponte didn't hesitate for a moment and immediately chose a very promising subject which had become one of the most fashionable and popular theatrical entertainments on the continent: the story of Don Juan.

The story had been conceived originally by the Spaniard Tirso de Molina in the 17th century. In 1787 alone five different versions of this story had been put on the stage. Da Ponte's libretto was a combination of two versions of the story produced that year in Venice.

Mozart arrived in Prague on October 1, 1787 and had already completed most of the score. The premiere was planned for October 14th. But they weren't ready in time and *Figaro* was played for the visit of the Prince and the Archduchess. There were difficulties at the rehearsals and one of the singers became ill. There are all sorts of legends surrounding the overture. Mozart supposedly wrote it the night before the premiere and the orchestra had to play it by sight. The ink was supposed to have been still wet. The fact is, however, that Mozart's new opera was extremely demanding and difficult to play so that some of the artists simply weren't up to it.

When it was finally first performed on October 29, 1787, it became an enormous success. A Prague newspaper reported: "Experts and musicians all agree that nothing like this has ever been performed in Prague before. Herr Mozart conducted himself and he was cheered enthusiastically from all sides both when he appeared as well as when the performance was over. The unusually large audience showed his popularity."

In Vienna da Ponte received a letter from the Prague opera director that is supposed to have said, "Evviva da Ponte! Evviva Mozart! The management and the artists feel very lucky. So long as you two live, poverty will never cross the threshold of our theater."

Lorenzo da Ponte is one of the most fascinating figures of the age. In the coursed of his extremely eventful life he changed from a Jew to being a Catholic, from a priest to a bon vivant, from a court poet in Vienna to a professor of Italian literature in New York. He wrote countless opera libretti and also worked for Mozart's biggest rival, Salieri. But his posthumous fame is based on the three most renowned Mozart operas: *The Marriage of Figaro, Così fan tutte* and *Don Giovanni.*

Even more adventurous than the life of da Ponte was the biography of the man who in his own life was the incarnation of the Don Juan figure – Giacomo Casanova. He was a Venetian and had known da Ponte from childhood. After having studied law and theology, he roamed restlessly throughout Europe. He visited the courts of Frederick the Great, Joseph II and Catherine the Great. He was a legend in his own time and became famous for having escaped from the infamous "lead chambers" in which the Venetians had imprisoned him. His later years were spent more quietly at Dux Castle as the librarian of Count Waldstein. His memoirs are of enormous interest for cultural history, but are famous for the descriptions of his erotic adventures.

Casanova left behind a revised version of the sextet in the second act of *Don Giovanni.* It could be that da Ponte himself inspired Casanova to this literary exercise. There is, however no historical evidence for Casanova having either collaborated on the libretto or attended the premiere. Equally unsubstantiated is Alfred Meissner's account of a personal meeting between Mozart and Casanova.

NORBERT BITTNER
Stage Design for *Don Giovanni*, 1817
*Copper engraving, 24.5 x 20.5 cm*
*Cologne, University,*
*Institute for Theater Studies*

The stage designs of Norbert Bittner
are the oldest visualizations we have
of a *Don Giovanni* production. They
are from the Romantic period, the age
which first began to realize how many
layers of meaning the opera has and
that this "drama giocosa" , this "cheer-
ful drama", has at the same time a
comic and a deeply serious side, both
of which have to be reflected on the
stage.

JOHANN ERNST MANSFELD
Post-Charte der k.k. Erblande von
Goerg Ignaz v. Mezburg, n.d.
*Print on paper and linen, 154 x 103 cm*
*(reduced to 102 x 68.2 cm)*
*Technisches Museum, Vienna*

This map of the stagecoach routes of
the Habsburg monarchy shows the
route Mozart took on his journey to
Prague for the *Don Giovanni* premiere
in 1787.

THOMAS MORSE
Portrait of Lorenzo da Ponte, n.d.
*Oil on canvas, 75 x 64 cm*
*New York Yacht Club*

The Venetian Lorenzo da Ponte was of
Jewish origins, but in 1763 he converted to Catholicism along with his
father and brothers. He was ordained
a priest in 1773, but, because of
numerous love affairs, he was forced
by the Inquisition to flee Italy.
He arrived in Vienna via Dresden.
Antonio Salieri was able to get him a
position at court. From then until
1791, he wrote some 40 opera libretti
for composers such as Antonio Salieri
or Vincente Martin y Soler. He
became famous, however, through
his texts for the Mozart operas, *The
Marriage of Figaro, Don Giovanni* and
*Così fan tutte*. In 1791 he lost his position as the result of a court intrigue.
He first moved to London and then
emigrated to New York in 1805.
There, he became a professor of Italian literature and helped to make
opera popular in America. His memoirs are an important, if not exactly
impartial, source of information about
Mozart.

ANONYMOUS
Portrait of Giacomo Casanova, n.d.
*Copper engraving, 15 x 10.5 cm*
*Dux Castle*

The Venetian Giacomo Casanova
(1725–1798) studied theology and law
and spent his life traveling through
Europe. He spent time at the courts
of Frederick the Great, Joseph II and
Catherine the Great. In 1785 this
adventurer and bon vivant became
librarian of Count Waldstein in Dux
and remained in the count's castle
until his death. His memoirs of enormous importance for cultural history
and have become famous for their
descriptions of his erotic adventures.

## THE REQUIEM AND MOZART'S DEATH

In July, 1791 a messenger brought Mozart an anonymous letter. In it, he was offered good payment for a requiem mass. Around the same time the Bohemian diet commissioned him to complete an opera by early September to celebrate the coronation of Leopold II as King of Bohemia. Mozart accepted the commission and composed La Clemenza di Tito. The requiem mass would have to wait. After all, at the same time he was also completing another commission (*The Magic Flute*) and that had to be ready by September 30.

At the end of August Mozart and his wife traveled to Prague for the coronation. When he returned to Vienna, he began to work intensively on the requiem. His physical condition got better. In between, he composed the "lesser" Masonic Cantata (KV 623) and directed it personally as part of a Masonic celebration on November 18th.

The enthusiastic reception this work received put him in an excellent mood and for a while he went back to the requiem and worked energetically. But already by November 20th he was so exhausted that he became bedridden. He complained of swelling and stomach pains. His physicians used the customary treatments of the time: bloodletting and cupping glasses. This treatment merely weakened him further. Despite this, he continued to work on the requiem mass until the end.

A contemporary witness reports on Mozart's unbroken creative power even on his death bed: *Even on the day before his death, he had the score of the Requiem brought to his bed and (it was two in the afternoon) he sang the alto part himself. His friend Schack sang the soprano part (as he always did); Mozart's brother-in-law sang the tenor and Gerle (later a bass at the Mannheim theatre) sang the bass part. They had just reached the first bars of the "Lacrimosa" when Mozart began to weep bitterly. He put the score to one side and was dead eleven hours later.*

Mozart died on December 5, 1791. His wife Constanze did her best to submit a completed score in order to make sure of getting the rest of the promised fee. Mozart's assistant, Franz Xaver Süssmayer completed the requiem in February, 1792. The score was sent to the anonymous patron who had ordered it. The riddle of his identity had been cleared up in the meantime. The commission had come from Count Walsegg von Stuppach. He was an amateur composer himself and had wanted to pass off Mozart's work as his own as a monument to the memory of his dead wife.

With Mozart's *Requiem* it is much like with his sickness and death: People just can't seem to leave it alone. Musicologists are still trying to figure out which notes were written by whom and have produced all sorts of "revisions" to show that they alone have sufficient empathy to sense exactly which parts are by Mozart. In our own day, physicians and pathologists have come up with a whole host of new names for the deadly disease that Mozart's physician called "enflamed fever": bronchopneumonia, renal failure, streptococcal infection, Schönlein-Henoch-Syndrom or bloodletting.

Posterity will also probably always enjoy speculating about the 'true reasons' for the early death of this genius. And so there will always be Mozart fans who quite seriously ask themselves. "Did Mozart kill himself by trying to cure his venereal disease with mercury?" "Did his rival Antonio Salieri poison him because he couldn't bear Mozart's superior talent?" "Or was Mozart's fellow mason Franz Hofdemel the poisoner?" After all, his wife probably had an affair with Mozart. And only one day after Mozart's death didn't he severely injure her and then cut his own throat?

It seems inevitable that truly great minds leave behind more questions than answers and it may be their way of reminding us of more essential questions. But one thing is certain: We will never hear enough of Mozart's music.

WOLFGANG AMADEUS MOZART
*Requiem* KV 626
First page of the "Dies Irae" of
the working score handwritten by
Mozart and Eybler, 1791
*Musical manuscript, 65 x 23.5 cm*
*ÖNB, Music Collection*

In July of 1791 Mozart accepted a
commission for a requiem, probably
because he needed the money. The
opening "Requiem aeterna" with the
double fugue "Kyrie Eleison" was
written entirely by Mozart. Another
five sections, plus the "Dies Irae" are
also by him. During his sickness, his
pupil Joseph Eybler assisted him in
writing down the notes. The composition breaks off in the middle of the
"Lacrimosa". These are the last notes
of music that Mozart wrote.

WOLFGANG AMADEUS MOZART
*Requiem* KV 626
First page of the "Dies Irae" in the
finished score, copied by Süssmayr,
1792(?)
*Musical manuscript, 65 x 23.5 cm*
*ÖNB, Music Collection*

After Mozart's death, his widow Constanze asked Mozart's pupil, Süssmayr
(1766–1803) to complete the piece.
Süssmayr, who may well have had an
affair with Constanze, was, like
Eybler, a collaborator of Mozart's and
familiar with the sketches and plans
for the *Requiem*. He completed it in
1792. In the same year Gottfried van
Swieten had it performed in Vienna.
The 300 Ducats earned by the concert
were given to Constanze.

**BLOOD-LETTING APPARATUS**
*Vienna, mid-18th century*
*Object of brass and steel in a leather box,*
*7.2 x 4.2 x 2.5 cm*
*Mozarthaus Vienna*

FRANÇOIS GONORD
Franz Graf Walsegg, n.d.
*Silhouette, enlarged print*
*WstLB*

The man who anonymously commissioned a requiem from Mozart was Franz Joseph Count Walsegg-Stuppach (1763–1827). An amateur composer, he was well known for ordering compositions from professional composers and then passing them off as his own. He wanted to have Mozart's *Requiem* performed as his own composition in memory of his dead wife. The go-between in this deal was probably Mozart's creditor, Puchberg, who lived in the count's Viennese residence. The famous "gray messenger" who brought Mozart the commission and the fee was one of the count's servants. The rumor mills of posterity have turned this servant into Mozart's "messenger of death". After Süssmayr completed the work, Count Walsegg-Stuppach had it performed in the Wiener Neustadt in 1793.

Mozart became severely ill on November 29, 1791. Due to his fame, he was naturally treated by the best medical experts of the city. Dr. Thomas Franz Closset was the personal physician to the Chancellor, Prince Kaunitz, and also treated other members of the imperial court; Dr. Matthias von Sallaba later became head of Vienna's main hospital. Both men diagnosed an "enflamed rheumatic fever" but could not be of any help. The therapeutic possibilities of the time were very limited.

## THE MAGIC FLUTE

*It sounds so splendid …* is sung in the glockenspiel passage of the first finale of *The Magic Flute (Die Zauberflöte)*. This opera has, like no other, moved biographers to wishful thinking. Most of them think of it as a sort of secular swan-song, a synthesizing apotheosis or the return to a divine simplicity. And in fact there are few other works of Mozart where the non-musical intentions of the composer have been so emphasized. It is a work which combines the characteristics of fairy tales, folk theatre, the German Singspiel and grand opera.

Schikaneder asked Mozart, probably in the spring 1791, whether he could write an opera for the Freihaus-Theater. Schikaneder himself wrote the libretto in close collaboration with Mozart and they called it a "German opera in two acts". Mozart composed all summer long, but not always with enthusiasm. He wrote to his wife who was at a spa in Baden near Vienna: "… if I go to the piano and sing something from it, I have to stop immediately – it gets me too agitated. Basta!"

Schikaneder was a theater impresario, poet and actor who had known Mozart ever since 1780. His theatre was part of a complex of buildings named after Prince Starhemberg. Schikaneder also lived there along with two of the musicians who would perform *The Magic Flute* for the first time: Mozart's sister-in-law Josepha Hofer (the first "Queen of the Night") and her husband, the violinist Franz de Paula Hofer. Nearby, in the Schleifmühlgasse lived Franz Xaver Gerl, the first Sarastro. Mozart supposedly wrote parts of the opera in a little garden house in a courtyard near the theatre. This so-called "Salettl" now stands in the garden of the Mozarteum in Salzburg.

The first performance took place on September 30, 1791. There was nothing about it that seemed at all unusual at the time and the tickets were no more expensive than for any other play in the repertoire. The large expenditure for theatrical machinery was, however, unusual and *The Magic Flute* has been called a "machine comedy". The scene painters Joseph Gayl and Nessthaler supplied new sets. The cast was taken from the experienced ensemble of the house. As was customary with such troupes of performers, the whole family took part. Emanuel Schikaneder played Papageno and he'd written the role to suit his own abilities perfectly. Mozart conducted the premiere and it was a sensational success. In October alone, it was performed 24 times. In 1792 Schikaneder announced the 100th performance and in 1795 the 200th. By 1794, other productions were put on in Prague, Frankfurt, Munich, Hamburg and Berlin.

After the first performances Mozart wrote on October 17, 1791: "The house was just as full as always. But what pleases me most is the 'silent applause'." Did he mean by this the huge royalties this fairy tale opera had earned for him? In any case he died only two months later and was never able to enjoy the success of his last opera. Today, just as in the 18th century, audiences are still listening to that wondrous music that Eugène Ionesco called a "divine smile" and that Mozart brought to life in his *Magic Flute*.

Theater Program for the Premiere
of Mozart's opera *The Magic Flute*
(KV 620), September 30, 1791
*Print, 37.3 x 23.3 cm*
*Wien Museum*

Mozart conducted the premiere himself, sitting at the piano. Although the
scene painters Joseph Gayl and
Nesslthaler had made new sets, the
cast itself was taken from the house
ensemble. Franz Xaver Gerl who had
once been a boy soprano at the
Salzburg court sang the first Sarastro.
The tenor Benedikt Schack (who was
also the house composer) sang the
role of Tamino. The Queen of the
Night was sung by Mozart's sister-in-
law Maria Josepha Hofer and Mozart's
pupil Anna Gottlieb sang Pamina.
Papageno was portrayed by Emanuel
Schickaneder himself and Papagena
was sung by Barbara Gerl, the sister
of Franz Xaver. Urban Schickaneder
(Emanuel's older brother) was the
First Priest.

CHECKPOINTMEDIA
Installation: "The Magic Flute"

The multi-media combines various
productions to produce a whole new
visual experience.

"*...trouble and commotion...*"

## THE MOZART APARTMENT ON THE FIRST FLOOR

Visitors now enter the rooms where Mozart and his family actually lived. This is one of smartest, largest and most expensive apartments that Mozart ever had. The time he spent here was musically productive and successful.

Mozart's apartment is a place where we commemorate the composer. Managed now by Wien Museum, the apartment has contained various installations over the 60 years it has been open to the public. As no original furniture that belonged to Mozart has come down to us, visitors are invited to let their imagination run riot. How did Mozart live and work in these rooms? Who all lived here? What was it like in here? The Mozarts' apartment was a noisy, busy place with private concerts, billiard games, babies crying, dogs barking …

The new installation invites visitors to seek out Mozart – but does so without recreating his apartment using props. The rooms themselves are the authentic core of Mozart's apartment. Note their proportions and sight lines, their doors and windows.

*Representative, upmarket apartment, central location, piano
nobile, 4 rooms, 2 closets, annual rent of 450 guldens plus costs*

## DINING ROOM?

*Why the question mark? How much furniture did the Mozarts
have? How full was their apartment? Who was Gauckerl?*

It was September 29, 1784 when Wolfgang Amadeus and
Constanze Mozart, together with their nine-day-old son
Carl Thomas, moved into the "Camesina-Haus" in Domgasse where they would spend more than two-and-a-half
years. It was the ninth of a total of fourteen apartments
that Mozart lived in over ten years in Vienna – and it is
the only one still standing. Since moving to the imperial
city, Mozart moved house on average three times a year.
Mr. and Mrs. Mozart were now finally well off and wanted
a spacious apartment in keeping with the 28-year-old composer's station. In a short space of time, he had become
the darling of Viennese society. Space was needed to
accommodate guests and throw parties. The Mozarts had
never had a lovelier or more expensive apartment. The
annual rent was about 450 guldens – as much as Mozart
had earned in Salzburg in a year.

It cannot now be said with certainty what happened in
which rooms, even if written sources such as letters, memoirs etc. and the ground plan permit likely suppositions.
Nevertheless, descriptions such as "guest room" or "study"
come with questions marks attached. It seems certain
where the kitchen was: in the very first room where there
is a centuries-old oven. Following the installation of an
elevator shaft, the former kitchen can now only be imagined. Why is the kitchen at the start of the tour? Because
visitors to the Mozarthaus now enter the apartment
through the former servants' entrance. The entrance for
"distinguished persons" was on the opposite side of the
apartment.

When the Mozarts moved in, there were three of them.
Their son, Carl August, spent the first 18 months of his life

here. In 1786, a second son was born but he died only a few weeks later. At least three servants lived in the apartment – and visiting guests besides. There were the family pets, too: a dog called "Gauckerl" and a songbird called "Stahrl".

A key that enables us to picture Mozart's apartment furnished and full of life is the inventory of his last apartment in Rauhensteingasse that he lived in before his death in 1791. An enlarged detail from his estate is shown here; it lists furniture and other household effects. It is not known when individual pieces came into Mozart's possession, of course. As the apartment in Rauhensteingasse was also quite large, it can be compared with the apartment in today's "Mozarthaus Vienna". It can be assumed that most of the furniture listed in the estate was bought for the apartment in the "Mozarthaus", as the apartments where the Mozarts lived before 1784 were all considerably smaller.

The tour starts with a model of the apartment; toy-sized furniture based on the above-mentioned inventory stands beside it. If one imagines it placed throughout the various rooms, it is easy to guess how much furniture the Mozart family had – and how cramped it must have been here.

Yet there is something authentic to be seen here, too: every room contains a piece of furniture or a utensil from late 18th-century Vienna, although none belonged to Mozart himself. In the catalog each one is annotated "From Mozart's time". These exhibits are based on his estate and indicate the likely purpose of each room. As the first room described here was off the kitchen, it may be assumed that it was the dining room. The 18th-century item on display is a porcelain fruit dish.

**Sperrs-RELATION.**

Todenfall
für der Stadt!

Namen des verstorbenen H. Wolfgang Amadeus
Mozard

Condition K. K. Kapellmeister, und Kammer Compositeur

Stand verheurathet, Alter 36 Jahre

Wohnung Nro 970. in der Rauhensteingassen
im kleinen Kaiserhause

Sterb-Tag den 5t Dec: 791.

Nachgelassener Ehegatt Constanz Ein Gebohrne

The Estate of
Wolfgang Amadeus Mozart, 1791
*Print and autograph, 37 x 23 cm*
*WstLA*

A few days after Mozart's death, this
list of his possessions was compiled
by a city official in the presence of
Constanze Mozart. The document
provides some insights into how the
Mozart family lived and what they
owned. Besides books, writings and
textiles, all Mozart's household goods
are listed here room by room. This list
is therefore invaluable for any imagi-
nary reconstruction of Mozart's apartment.

ANONYMOUS
Wolfgang Amadeus Mozart, 1803
*Gouache-tempera on parchment,*
*15.3 x 10.4 cm*
*Wien Museum*

Mozart's sister Maria Anna (Nannerl),
Reichsfreiin von Berchtold zu Sonnenburg, probably had this portrait
painted in Salzburg in 1803; the artist
is unknown. Maria Anna lent the artist
a Mozart family portrait, probably
done by Johann Nepomuk Della
Croce in 1780/81, and other Mozart
portraits in her possession, as models.
Mozart is shown holding a book with
his left hand in such a way that he can
read his own monogram: AM (= Amadeus Mozart).

Constanze Mozart, née Weber
(1762–1842), 1782
*Lithograph after an oil painting
by Joseph Lange, 19th century,
19.9 x 15.2 cm
Wien Museum*

The painter and actor Joseph Lange,
the husband of Constanze's sister
Aloysia, produced this portrait of his
sister-in-law the year she married
Mozart in Vienna's Stephansdom
(1782). This lithograph may have been
produced early in the 19th century.

J. E. MANSFELD AFTER
JOHANN CHRISTIAN BRAND
Bird seller, 1775/76
*Colored engraving (detail)
Wien Museum*

In spring 1784, Mozart acquired a
songbird called "Stahrl" or "Staar". It
was said to be able to sing the rondo
from the piano concerto in G major
for Barbara Ployer (KV 453). A few
weeks after the Mozarts moved out
of this apartment, the bird died. On
June 4, 1787 Mozart composed an
obituary to "Stahrl" that is not without parody.

Mozart's sons Carl Thomas and
Franz Xaver Wolfgang, c. 1798
*Engraving after an oil painting
by Hans Hansen (1769–1828),
16.6 x 12.1 cm
Wien Museum*

Of the Mozarts' six children, only
these two sons survived childhood.
Carl Thomas (1784–1858) was only
nine days old when he moved into
the apartment at Domgasse 5 with his
parents. After 1805, he studied music
in Milan, but gave up any thoughts
of a career in music, choosing instead
to become a civil servant. His brother
Franz Xaver Wolfgang (1791–1844),
later called "Wolfgang Amadeus
Mozart Sohn", was born a few
months before his father's death.
He, too, became a musician.

JOSEPH DANIEL HUBER
Birds'-eye view of the center
of Vienna, 1785
*Engraving and etching, 167 x 176 cm*
*Wien Museum*

This plan by the military cartographer
Joseph Daniel Huber (1730/31–1788)
was produced as part of a proposed
extension to the city. Now considered
to be one of the most important
images of historical Vienna, it shows
that elegant Trattnerhof on Graben,
where Mozart lived before moving to
Domgasse, was only a few hundred
paces from his new home.

QUIRIN MARK AFTER
JOHANN CHRISTIAN BRAND
Seller of hare skins, 1775/76
*Colored engraving (detail)*
*Wien Museum*

While traveling to Prague in January
1787, Wolfgang Amadeus and his wife
passed the time by inventing silly
names for themselves and their
friends. Mozart became Pùnkititititi,
Constanze SchablaPumfa. Mozart's
dog, "Gauckerl", is also mentioned in
this context; he became Schamanuzky.
It is not known when Mozart got him
or what breed of dog he was.

*From Mozart's time*
Fruit dish by Wiener
Porzellanmanufaktur, 1788
*Embossed "G" (= Markus Klampferer,*
*embosser?), 11 x 22.5 x 29.5 cm*
*Wien Museum*

Mozart's estate lists "60 pcs. misc.
porcelain" as well as the "small number of usual kitchen utensils". A fruit
dish like this may have been among
them.

## GUEST ROOM?

*Where did Mozart's father Leopold live? Did Mozart open his home to musicians visiting Vienna? Did he have any assistants?*

The Mozarts' social life was centered on the suite of rooms that looked out on Domgasse. These rooms were directly accessible from outside and appear to have served as space for living in, accommodating guests and teaching pupils. If this was where Mozart gave music lessons, the room of course contained a piano.

Accompanied by his pupil Heinrich Marchand, Mozart's father visited for two months in 1785. Leopold passed comment on the organizational skills of his daughter-in-law Constanze: "... housekeeping in terms of food and drink is economical in the highest degree."

It was mainly musicians visiting Vienna and composition students from outside town who lodged here for longer periods of time. From 1785, the 20-year-old Englishman Thomas Attwood spent a good year in Vienna and studied composition under Mozart. His pupils often worked as assistants: they wrote parts, copied music, performed piano compositions that had been submitted or accompanied Mozart in duets.

A child prodigy was among the long-stay visitors. Early in 1786, Mozart accepted the 7-year-old son of a musician from Pressburg as a pupil and gave him music lessons free of charge: it was Johann Nepomuk Hummel. As he later recalled, he spent almost two years with the Mozarts in Vienna. Hummel became an important virtuoso pianist who throughout his life was influenced by his mentor's music. As a child, then, he was a temporary member of the Mozart family and fully involved in the Mozart music-making business.

NANETTE ROSENZWEIG
Johann Nepomuk Hummel
at the piano, c. 1800
*Miniature, 6,7 cm*
*Düsseldorf, Goethe-Museum, Anton-und-*
*Katharina-Kippenberg-Stiftung*

Early in 1786, the violinist and conductor Johann Hummel (1754–1828)
and his son Johann Nepomuk
(1778–1837) visited Mozart at home in
Domgasse. Hummel senior later
recalled the meeting: "Well, sit down
at the piano and show what you can
do", Mozart said to Nepomuk. From
among his music, he produced some
small things by Bach that he had
worked hard at and placed them in
front of him. Mozart let him be and
he started to play … When my boy
finished the Bach, Mozart placed a not
altogether easy piece of his own in
front of him … It went very well … A
short while later, my Nepomuk moved
into the Mozarts' home where he was
kept as one of their own." Johann
Nepomuk Hummel became an excellent pianist and later worked as music
director at the courts of Stuttgart and
Weimar, among others.

ANONYMOUS
Thomas Attwood, n.d.
*Oil on canvas, facsimile*
*Royal College of Music, London*

From London, Attwood studied music
theory and composition under Mozart
from summer/autumn 1785 until
August 1786. Back in England,
Attwood (1765–1838) went on to
become an organist, composer and
conductor. He wrote church music,
songs, piano compositions, and
operas.

Exercise sheet by Thomas Attwood
with Mozart's corrections
*Autograph, 22.5 x 32 cm*
*Permission, British Library, London*

The sheet is taken from Attwood's
exercise book and contains corrections by Mozart. In class, Mozart and
his pupil spoke mostly Italian, but
Mozart also made an effort to practice
his English. Written presumably after
August 23, 1785, Mozart wrote the
following to his pupil: "This after
noon I am not at home, therefore I
pray you to come to morrow at three
& a half."

*From Mozart's time*
Chair, late 18th century
*Wood with inlaid work,*
*91.5 x 46 x 53.5 cm*
*Hofmobiliendepot – Möbel Museum Wien*

When Mozart died, the family owned
18 chairs: six each covered in canvas,
linen and cotton twill, and damask.
Despite its inlaid work, the simple
style of this chair indicates that it
stood in a middle-class home, rather
than an aristocratic one.

## SALON? GAMES ROOM?
*Where was the billiard table? Where was music played?*
*How many guests attended Mozart's private concerts?*

Mozart loved to play with words and music, but also with cards and billiards. In Vienna at the time, billiards was a status symbol that represented a wealthy and luxurious lifestyle. "He was passionate about billiards and had a billiard table at home", recalled Michael O'Kelly, a tenor and friend of Mozart's, in his memoirs. It was difficult to beat him at the game. Mozart often had visitors at home, and they did full justice to the punch on offer. They were also there to hear music, of course: Mozart "gave Sunday concerts which I never missed".

This gives rise to some interesting speculation: if this is the largest room on the "public" side of the building looking onto Domgasse, it can be assumed that the billiard table stood here. The size of the room suggests that private concerts were also held in it. It appears to have been common practice just to move chairs from room to room depending on requirements. This might then have been a games room that – besides other uses – was sometimes turned into a domestic "concert hall". Playing – whether of games or music – is brought to mind here for visitors.

What might have this room looked like furnished? An experiment is intended to aid visitors' imaginations. The model maker Augustin Fischer has built miniature examples of typical furniture of the time – not the splendid sort found in palaces, but plainer stuff such as was found in middle-class homes – and arranged them around a billiard table. The style of the furniture is a mix of rococo and classical, as even then people did not always own only modern furniture. The scale model was photographed by Benjamin Eichhorn and was transferred onto a large-scale image that now hangs on an end wall of the room.

A gaming table from Mozart's time stands at the center of the room. In view of the large numbers of visitors, a historical billiard table would have been too bulky here.

There is every reason to believe that the room also contained a special table for board, card, and dice games.

The second main motif of this room is chamber music – and therefore Mozart's adoration of Joseph Haydn, his senior by twenty-five years. Haydn visited in mid February 1785 to attend a private concert. The first violin was played by a world-class violin virtuoso, Mozart's father Leopold. Wolfgang played viola, and the Barons Tinti from Salzburg played second violin and cello. They played the string quartets known as the "Haydn Quartets". Like many works from around this time, the quartets were composed without being commissioned. They show just how much Mozart had become a freelance artist in the modern sense. Only after auditioning them for Haydn, who had a very high opinion of Mozart's talent, did Mozart dedicate the work to him. If all the indications are right, Mozart received Haydn's "official approval" in this room. Of course, it might also just have been an enjoyable evening's entertainment.

It is worthwhile to look out the window on the right in this room. The view is of Blutgasse whose buildings have hardly changed since Mozart's day. The last house on the right-hand side of the lane is the "Deutschordenshaus" where Mozart, still in the service of Salzburg, had first taken lodgings in Vienna with his few possessions in March 1781.

**JOHANN ERNST MANSFELD**
(1738–1796)
Joseph Haydn, n.d.
*Engraving, 26.6 x 19 cm*
*Wien Museum*

Joseph Haydn and Mozart held each other in great esteem. Haydn was probably a frequent visitor to Mozart's home in Domgasse and played music there with his host. One evening in February 1785, Haydn said to Leopold, full of admiration: "As an honest man before God, I tell you that your son is the greatest composer known to me in person or by name."

**WOLFGANG A. MOZART**
Six string quartets, op. X, 1785
*First edition, title page and first page,*
*33.5 x 24.2 cm*
*WStLB, Musiksammlung*

Written between winter 1782 and January 1785, Mozart's series of six string quartets (KV 387, 421, 428, 458, 464 and 465) was first published by Artaria in Vienna in September 1785. In a letter to his father in January 1785, Mozart writes that, the previous Saturday, he had auditioned the six quartets he had sold to Artaria for 100 ducats in front of his dear friend Haydn and other good friends. Mozart dedicated these quartets to Joseph Haydn in Italian.

HIERONYMUS LÖSCHENKOHL
Michael O'Kelly, n.d.
*Engraved silhouette, 8 x 5 cm*
*Wien Museum*

The Irish tenor and composer Michael O'Kelly (or Michael Kelly; 1762–1826) stayed in Vienna from 1783 to 1787 and was a frequent visitor to the Mozarts' home. At the first performance of *The Marriage of Figaro* on May 1, 1786, he took the parts of the music teacher Basilio and the judge Don Curzio.

*From Mozart's time*
Playing cards published by Johann Norbert Hoffmann, Vienna, c. 1800
*Colored woodcut on cardboard,*
*each 8.6 x 5.7 cm*
*Wien Museum*

*From Mozart's time*
Gaming table, late 18th century
*Varieties of wood, inlay, 77 x 83 x 57 cm*
*Wien Museum*

Mozart's estate lists a number of "hard tables", including one in the billiard room. Like many of their contemporaries, Mozart and Constanze enjoyed playing parlor games such as billiards, cards, or guessing games, so there is reason to believe that one of these tables was used for games. This multi-purpose gaming table originally had a top that could be removed if necessary; it was suitable for board games such as chess, checkers, nine men's morris and trictrac, today's backgammon. At opposite corners of the table, there are two pullout leaves on which drinking glasses were presumably placed.

### SERVANTS' ROOM? ANTEROOM?

*Where did the servants live? How cold was it in the apartment?*
*Where was the main entrance?*

Two narrow passages with windows overlooking the courtyard give rise to the question of where the servants slept –
for the Mozart family did not live alone. They always had
at least three servants around them: a cook, a maid and
Mozart's manservant Joseph. In the 18th century, servants
did not have their own, permanent living quarters. The
cook and the maid probably slept in the kitchen. At least
we know that was the case in the last apartment Mozart
lived in in Rauhensteingasse. His estate lists "two soft
beds" in the kitchen.

But where did Joseph sleep? An "ordinary servant's bed"
is listed in the inventory, but where was it kept? It is certainly possible that Joseph made up his bed every night
in one of these passageways and put it away again in the
morning.

The exhibit from Mozart's time chosen by the curators
of Wien Museum is a simple, iron candlestick. It reminds
us of the variety of duties a manservant had to perform
then: he was in charge of lighting – from when his masters
rose in the morning to lighting the way home for visitors
late at night – as well as for heating.

A stove, possibly 18th century, is still extant, but we
should not imagine that this was a "well-tempered" home.
It was freezing even in upmarket apartments back then.
On a February day in 1785, Leopold wrote to his daughter
in St. Gilgen: "As I write this, it is already 5 of the clock.
It is snowing terribly and the wind is surprising and is
tearing through these poorly-heated rooms."

The fact that tradesmen kept coming and going certainly
contributed to the noise in the apartment. Leopold complained in a letter that he could find no peace to write
because either the masseur or the floor polisher was dancing around the room. The barber arrived in the morning

to shave the gentlemen; traders and piano tuners, delivery boys or knife grinders came and went.

This room is described as an anteroom because of the large door in the next room. When the Mozarts lived here, it was the main entrance for them and their distinguished visitors.

Servant. Un Laquais, 1777
*Engraving no. 30 from: Jakob Adam,*
*Abbildungen des gemeinen Volks zu Wien.*
*/ Les Portraits du commun peuple a*
*Vienna (Images of the common people of*
*Vienna), 17.8 x 11.3 cm*
*Wien Museum*

While traveling to Prague in January 1787, Mozart invented the name of "Sagadaratà" for his manservant Joseph, presumably because he often used to say "Sag' ich dir auch!" (I tell you!) at the end of his sentences. Even in 1791, Mozart mentions Joseph in letters to Constanze. The servant illustrated here is the work of the draughtsman and engraver Jakob Adam (1748–1811). It is part of a market criers' series and is a stylized image.

*From Mozart's time*
Candlestick, Vienna, 18th century
*Wrought iron*
*Wien Museum*

Mozart's estate lists several "lights". While some of them were used solely to light the billiard table, others were portable and used in different rooms as and when they were needed. This candlestick had an adjustable sleeve to suit the length of the candle. A rectangular base on four feet prevented the wax from dripping onto the surrounding furniture.

### STUDY?

*Did Mozart work night and day? Did he earn a lot?*
*How many faces were there to him?*

This is the room where the opera *The Marriage of Figaro*
was created – if our assumption that Mozart's piano and
desk stood here is correct. The time Mozart spent in the
apartment in Domgasse was among the most productive of
his life. Deadlines and pressure were the order of the day;
his output and the stress arising from it were high. He
would have meetings to discuss projects, outline ideas,
copy out parts and music, and rehearse piano parts. When
his father Leopold arrived in Vienna on February 11, 1785,
the day of the first performance of the piano concerto in
D minor, KV 466, he was rather surprised to see that the
music had not yet been copied out in full and that his son
"had not even had time to play the rondo through once
because he was overseeing the copying of the music".

From October 1785, Mozart began to work intensively
on *Figaro,* working alongside the librettist Lorenzo da
Ponte in the first few weeks. The libretto and the music
appear to have been produced almost in tandem: "as I
wrote the words, he set them to music" (da Ponte). The
closer the premiere came, the tenser and more nervous the
composer became. Would the censor really pass this piece
with its criticism of the aristocracy? After all, it was mod-
eled on a contemporary comedy by Beaumarchais that
advocated equality for all. "Mozart was as volatile as gun-
powder", recalled the Irish tenor Michael O'Kelly, who
sang the role of Basilio at the premiere on May 1, 1786 in
the Burgtheater on Michaelerplatz. The performances
finally went ahead as planned. Lorenzo da Ponte had
translated the charged subject matter into Italian,
abridged and depoliticized it.

In the intense six month period during which Mozart
worked on *Figaro* "in a rush" (Leopold Mozart), countless
other works were produced at the same time: the musical
comedy *Der Schauspieldirektor*, three piano concertos, the

*Maurerische Trauermusik,* a piano rondo, two Masonic songs, a sonata for piano and violin, a number of operatic interludes as well as small works for wind instruments. It was calculated at the time that Mozart averaged an unbelievable six pages of twelve staves a day. To illustrate this achievement, the six-page-long manuscript of choral song no. 8 "Giovani liete" from *Figaro* is on display here.

How did Mozart cope with this surprising workload? Noise and chaos appear not to have bothered him terribly much. From letters from the 1780s, it is known that Mozart often composed until after midnight – even after having his friends round! From 1784, Mozart tried to give piano lessons only in the afternoons "to keep mornings free for composing".

The scholar Volkmar Braunbehrens has calculated Mozart's annual income at between 3,000 and 4,000 guldens; in other words, it was close to that of a *Hofrat*. Besides piano lessons and publishing, his most important sources of income were the takings from the concerts at which he played his own works. Besides "salon concerts" organized by patrons in their palaces and homes, it was mainly public concerts ("academies") that were of major importance for his income.

In the time Mozart lived in Domgasse, he also organized his own concerts. In 1785 alone, he hired the hall in the "Mehlgrube" municipal casino on Neuer Markt no less than five times. With pride, Leopold Mozart described in a letter to his daughter how, on February 11, 1785, "a large gathering of persons of rank" was present in the hall for the first performance of the piano concerto in D minor. He was also impressed by his son's business sense: for "the six Lenten concerts, each person pays a gold sovereign or 3 ducats. It is at the Mehlgrube where for the hall he pays only half a gold sovereign each time. The concert was incomparable, the orchestra splendid …" After deduction of costs, Mozart was left with a significant profit. For each performance, Mozart's piano had to be carried out the house – meaning several times a month. The space where

Mozart worked was therefore busy all the time. Leopold wrote that it was impossible to describe all the "trouble and noise" he found there. The Viennese piano-maker Anton Walter acquired the grand piano that once stood here; it is now in Mozart's birthplace in Salzburg. What has not survived is a specially made "forte piano pedale": this was an auxiliary instrument located beneath the grand piano, and was based on a pedal-board harpsichord. Mozart used its pedals to improvise during concerts.

A number of portraits of Mozart hang in the room. With few exceptions, they were copied after other portraits, some even only after his death. These are therefore "second-hand" portraits that prove the popularity of the composer and virtuoso pianist. They mark the transition from more or less authentic to reproduced images of him.

Act I, 8 chorus: Giovani liete, 1785
*Autograph from »The Marriage of Figaro«,*
*22.5 x 32 cm*
*Staatsbibliothek zu Berlin*

HIERONYMUS LÖSCHENKOHL
Wolfgang Amadeus Mozart, 1785
*Engraved silhouette, 8.1 x 5 cm*
*Wien Museum*

The engraver, painter, art dealer, and
publisher Hieronymus Löschenkohl
(1753–1807) came from the Rhine-
land, and was active in Vienna after
1779. Besides a great many engravings
of contemporary events, he produced
mainly silhouettes of actors, musicians, and scientists. Löschenkohl
designed this silhouette in 1785 for a
theater calendar. It was used as a
model for numerous reproductions.

JOHANN ADAM DELSENBACH
(1687–1765)
"Die Mehlgrube", n.d.
*Colored Engraving, 25.9 x 36.6 cm*
*Wien Museum*

The "Mehlgrube" in the 1780s was a
popular middle-class venue for music
and dancing. In February and March
1785, Mozart gave several successful
subscription concerts there. The
building stood on the corner of Neuer
Markt 5 and Kärntner Strasse 22, and
was demolished at the end of the 19th
century. It is now the location of the
Hotel Ambassador.

LEONHARD POSCH
Wolfgang Amadeus Mozart, 1788
*Plaster relief (copy), 8.2 x 6.9 x 1.5 cm*
*Wien Museum*

From Tyrol, Leonhard Posch
(1750–1831) was a wax embosser,
engraver of medals, sculptor, and
friend of Mozart. From 1788 to 1790
in Vienna, he created several portrait
reliefs of Mozart that were used,
among others, by Johann Georg
Mansfeld, Clemens Kohl, and Johann
Joseph Neidl as models for their own
portraits of him.

DORIS STOCK
Wolfgang Amadeus Mozart, 1789
*Intaglio engraving after a silverpoint*
*drawing, 45.4 x 33.5 cm*
*Wien Museum*

En route to Berlin in 1789, Mozart
stopped off at Dresden where several
times in mid-April he visited Christian
Gottfried Körner, a friend of Friedrich
Schiller. Körner's sister-in-law Doris
Stock (1760–1832), an aunt of the
poet Theodor Körner and a talented
amateur artist, thus had the opportunity to capture Mozart's likeness.

STUPPI
"Giovanni Mozart", c. 1791
*Lithograph, 25.5 x 17.4 cm*
*Wien Museum*

LEGRUM (?)
"Mozart, célèbre compositeur,
né en 1756, mort en 1791", c. 1791
*Lithograph, Paris, 24.5 x 18.6 cm*
*Wien Museum*

P. ROHRBACH
"Mozart", 1863
*Lithograph, Berlin, 50.8 x 41.1 cm*
*Wien Museum*

*From Mozart's time*
Musical clock, c. 1790/91
*Wood with gilt finish, 82 x 60 x 40 cm*
*Wien Museum*

Mozart's estate also lists "1 clock and
clockwork in a gilt casing". The clock
shown here, made c. 1790, plays several melodies, of which one is said to
be by Mozart. It is a variation of
KV 616 that in the composer's own
autograph list of works is called "an
andante for a cylinder in a small
organ"; it is dated May 4, 1791. This
clock was kept for many years in
Müller's Building beside the Rother
Turm. The owner of the art gallery
there, Graf Deym, was an admirer of
Mozart, and he commissioned this
piece from him. It is fairly certain that
Mozart composed his piece for a
clock such as this – if not this very
one.

### BEDROOM?
*Did Mozart live in a designer apartment? Who was Camesina?*

At the end of the suite of rooms lies a room whose rich decoration comes as a surprise because it would be better suited to an aristocrat's palace than a middle-class home: pinkish-gray stuccowork imitates expensive marble facing. A relief on the ceiling depicts Flora, the goddess of flowers, among amoretti weaving garlands.

This opulent decorative scheme brings to mind the early history of the building that in Mozart's day was known as the "Camesina-Haus". Around 1720, it was acquired and refurbished by the court stuccoist Albert Camesina. In the 18th century, stuccoists were not just craftsmen who knew how to use stucco. They were highly gifted and admired artists who created the kind of elaborate, three-dimensional ornamentation on walls and ceilings without which 18th century interior decoration would be unthinkable. This room may have been decorated a short while later. It was probably the room in which Mozart displayed his abilities to potential clients from the Church and the aristocracy.

A marble relief of Emperor Charles VI above the door complements Camesina's accomplished interior design. The relief is surrounded by gilded horns of plenty and probably originates from the workshop of the sculptor Paul Strudel. When Mozart moved in in 1784, these rich decorations were already over 50 years old. The house was still owned by the Camesina family: Mozart's landlady was the daughter-in-law of the famous stuccoist.

Experts are divided as to how the room was used. Mozart's biographer Otto Erich Deutsch was convinced in 1965 that the composer used it as his study. Writing in his Mozart biography published in 2005, Martin Geck is more cautious: "This was possibly his study". In contrast, according to Walter Brauneis in the 1996 "Figarohaus" catalog: "The original use of this room can be imagined from how it extends into a plain alcove: this was the bedroom

in whose alcove there once stood a bed." A cradle and
a child's bed would have stood here too: Mozart's son
Carl Thomas was only nine days old when his father and
mother moved into the "Camesina-Haus". Their third
child was born here two years later in October 1786. He
was called Johann (Johannes) Thomas Leopold, but died
within a month.

CHRISTIAN SEYBOLD
Court stuccoist Albert Camesina,
c. 1740
*Oil on canvas, framed, 75.4 x 61.8 cm*
*Wien Museum*

Originally from Graubünden, stuccoist
Albert (or Alberto) Camesina (1675–
1756) settled in Vienna around 1710
and set himself up in business as a
master craftsman. In 1714, he became
court stuccoist and was involved in
the design of major Baroque buildings. In Vienna his work is seen at
Schloss Belvedere, the Altes Rathaus
and Deutschordenshaus, as well as in
the Karlskirche and Peterskirche.

*From Mozart's time*
Child's bed, c. 1780
*Walnut, 80.5 x 67 x 132 cm*
*Wien Museum*

According to the inventory of his
possessions at his death, Mozart left
a "marriage bed and 1 child's bed".
The late 18th century bed shown here
might have stood in a similar, middle-
class household. The lack of any decoration identifying it as a child's bed
is typical of the time; it appears more
to be a miniature version of an adult
bed.

*"… I want to have everything*
*that is good and genuine and*

*...beautiful ..."*

# Mozarthaus Vienna

## APPENDIX

## MOZART'S BIOGRAPHY

**1756** On January 27th Johann Chrysostomos Wolfgang Theophilus (lat. Amadeus) Mozart is born in Salzburg.

**1761** The five-year-old Mozart composes his very first works for piano (KV 1a–1f).

**1762** Leopold Mozart (1719–1787) takes his two child prodigies Maria Anna ("Nannerl", 1751–1829) and Wolfgang Amadeus to Munich for three weeks of guest appearances.

**1763** From September 18, 1762 to January 5, 1763 Leopold Mozart travels with his wife Anna Maria née Pertl (1720–1778) and the two children to Vienna and Bratislava.

**1763–66** The Mozart family travels to Paris, London and Den Haag.

**1766** The Mozart family has guest appearances in Paris for the second time.

**1767–69** The family gives concerts for the second time in Vienna.

**1768** Mozart completes his second "Singspiel" *Bastien und Bastienne* (KV 50).
On January 7th Mozart conducts a concert for the consecration of the Waisenhaus Church on the Rennweg in Vienna. The concert includes (among other works) his Mass (KV 47a) and his Offertorium (KV 47b) and was performed in the presence of the Empress Maria Theresia and her son, the future Joseph II.

**1769** Mozart becomes the unpaid third concertmaster of the Salzburg court orchestra.
From December 13<sup>th</sup> to March 28, 1771 he makes a first trip to Italy with his father.

**1770** In Rome Pope Clement XIV makes him a "Knight of the Golden Spur". In Milan his opera seria *Mitridate, Rè di Ponto* is performed for the first time.

**1771** Mozart once again travels to Italy with his father.

**1772** In August Mozart becomes first concertmaster of the Salzburg court orchestra and is given a salary.
A third journey to Italy takes Mozart and his father back to Milan. There, on the 26<sup>th</sup> of December his opera seria *Lucio Silla* has its premiere.

**1773** Together with his father, he makes a third visit to Vienna. That autumn the family moves from their old house in the Getreidegasse to the "Tanzmeisterhaus" on today's Makart-Platz.

**1774–75** Mozart travels with his father to Munich. His opera buffa *La finta giardiniera* (KV 196) is performed there for the first time on January 13, 1775.

The premiere of the serenata *Il re pastore* (KV 208) takes place in Salzburg. Mozart composes piano sonatas, serenades and the violin concerto in A Major (KV 219).

**1776** Mozart composes piano concerti, serenades (among them the "Haffner" Serenade, KV 284b), divertimenti, church sonatas and masses.

**1777** In August and at his own request, Mozart leaves the service of the Salzburg court. He travels with his mother to Mannheim and Paris.

**1778** The "Paris" Symphony (KV 297) is performed in the Tuileries for the first time.
On July 3rd Mozart's mother dies in Paris. The day after she is buried in the churchyard of St. Eustache.

**1779** In January Mozart returns to Salzburg. He becomes court organist and composes the "Coronation" Mass (KV 317) as well as other orchestral and liturgical music.

**1780** Mozart travels to Munich for rehearsals of his opera *Idomeneo, Rè di Creta, ossia: Ilia ed Idamante* and conducts the premiere on January 29, 1781.

**1781** Mozarts employer, the Prince-Archbishop Hieronymus, Count Colloredo commands him to leave Munich and be in Vienna on March 16th.
On May 9th he has a violent row with Colloredo.
On June 8th one of Colloredo's courtiers, Felix Count Arco (1743–1830) has a dispute with Mozart and gives him a kick in the pants. Now the composer decides that his time at the Salzburg court is definitely over. He moves to Vienna to live as a free-lance musician and composer. Between June and December Mozart attracts his first students: Marie Caroline Countess Thiennes de Rumbeke (1755–1812), Maria Wilhelmine Countess Thun-Hohenstein (1747–1800), Josepha Barbara Auernhammer (1758–1820) and Maria Theres(i)a von Trattner (1758–1793).

**1782** On July 26th *The Abduction from the Seraglio*
*(Die Entführung aus dem Serail)* is first performed at
the Burgtheater.
On August 4th Mozart marries Constanze Weber
(1762–1842) in St. Stephan's Cathedral. The newly-
wedded husband composes a series of piano concerti
and the "Haffner" Symphony (KV 385).

**1783** Their first child (Raimund Leopold) is born on
June 17th but dies already on August 19th. Mozart and
Constanze go to Salzburg from the end of July to November. The "Linzer" symphony (KV 425) is performed for
the first tine in Linz on November 4th.

**1784** On August 23rd Mozart's sister Nannerl marries
Johann Baptist Franz von Berchtold zu Sonnenburg
(1736–1801) in St. Gilgen.
September 21st is the birthday of their second son
Carl Thomas (died 1858 in Milan).
On September 29th the family moves into the Grosse
Schulerstrasse 8 / Domgasse (at that time house no. 846).
This was the most impressive of the 14 apartments the
Mozart family lived in during their time in Vienna.
Today this is the "Mozarthaus Vienna".

On December 14<sup>th</sup> Mozart is accepted into the Masonic Lodge "Benevolence".

**1785** From February 7<sup>th</sup> to April 25<sup>th</sup> Leopold lives with his son in the Schulerstrasse, today's "Mozarthaus Vienna".
Father and son meet Joseph Haydn. Mozart gives piano concerts in the presence of his father and, together, they make music at home.

**1786** Mozart's comedy *Der Schauspieldirektor* (KV 486) has its first performance at the Burgtheater. *The Marriage of Figaro* has its premiere on May 1<sup>st</sup>.
On October 18<sup>th</sup> Mozart's third child is born (Johannes Thomas Leopold). The child dies on November 15<sup>th</sup>.

**1787** From the 8<sup>th</sup> of January until mid February Mozart, Constanze and Franz de Paula Hofer (1755–1796) travel to Prague.
On January 17<sup>th</sup> *The Marriage of Figaro* is performed in his presence and it is an enormous success.
On Janury 19<sup>th</sup> is the first performance of the "Prague Symophony" (KV 504).
In April Ludwig van Beethoven (1770–1827) visits him in Vienna.
April 23<sup>th</sup>: Mozart leaves his home in the Domgasse.
On May 28<sup>th</sup> his father Leopold dies in Salzburg.
From October 1st to mid November Mozart and Constanze are in Prague.
On October 29<sup>th</sup> is the premiere of the drama giocoso *Il dissoluto punito ossia Il Don Giovanni.*
On December 27<sup>th</sup> Mozart's fourth child Theresia Konstantia Adelheid Friderika Maria Anna is born; the child dies six months later on June 29, 1788.

**1788** Mozart writes three symphonies (KV 553, 550, 551), chamber music and dance music.
On October 29th *Don Giovanni* (KV 524) has its Vienna premiere with new arias (KV 540 a–c).

**1789** From April 8th to June 4th Mozart travels to Berlin with Prince Karl Lichnowsky (1761–1814).
On November 16th Mozart's fifth child Anna Maria is born, but dies a few hours after her birth.
First performance of the clarinet quintet (KV 581) on December 22nd.

**1790** On January 26th the opera buffa *Così fan tutte* has its first performance.
February 20th: Joseph II dies.
From September 23rd until the beginning of November Mozart travels to Frankfurt with his brother-in-law Franz de Paula Hofer for the coronation of Leopold II.

**1791** On July 26th Mozart's sixth child (Franz Xaver Wolfgang) is born. The child dies in 1844 in Karlsbad.
From August 25/26th until mid-September Constanze, Mozart and his assistant and pupil Franz Xaver Süssmayr (1766–1803) are in Prague. There, on September 6th his opera seria *La Clemenza di Tito* is performed for the first time.
On September 30th in Vienna, Mozart's "German Opera" *The Magic Flute* has its premiere in the Freihaus Theater.
On November 20th Mozart becomes seriously ill. He is entrusted to the care of two prominent physicians, Dr. Thomas Franz Closset (1754–1813) and Dr. Thomas von Sallaba (1764–1797). Even on his deathbed, he continues work on the *Requiem* (KV 626).
At about one in the morning on December 5th he dies in his apartment in the Rauhensteingasse in Vienna.

SOURCES

Deutsch, Otto Erich (ed.): *Mozart. Die Dokumente seines Lebens* (= NMA X/34). Kassel 1961

Goes, Albrecht (ed.): *Mozart Briefe*. Frankfurt a.M. 1979

Klose, Dietrich: *"Komponirt ist schon alles – aber geschrieben noch nicht"*. *Mozart zum Vergnügen*. Stuttgart 2005

Köchel, Ludwig Ritter von: *Chronologisch-thematisches Verzeichnis sämtlicher Tonwerke Wolfgang Amadé Mozarts*. 8th edition, revised by Franz Giegling, Alexander Weinmann und Gerd Sievers. Wiesbaden 1983

Leopold, Silke (ed.): *"Guten Morgen, liebes Weibchen!"* *Mozarts Briefe an Constanze*. Kassel 2005

Mozart. *Briefe und Aufzeichnungen*. Complete edition, ed. by the Internationale Stiftung Mozarteum Salzburg, collected and commented by Wilhelm A. Bauer und Otto Erich Deutsch. Vol. I–IV. Kassel 1963

Mozart. *Eigenhändiges Werkverzeichnis* (= NMA X/33/Abt.l). Kassel 1991

*Mozart, WA/Bauer, Jutta* (eds.): Bona Nox. Hildesheim 2005

Rosenthal, Albi und Alan Tyson (eds.): *Mozart's Thematic Catalogue: A Facsimile*. British Library Stefan Zweig MS 63. Ithaca 1990

SECONDARY LITERATURE

Angermüller, Rudolph: *Mozart's Operas*. New York 1988

Angermüller, Rudolph: *Mozart 1485/86 bis 2003. Daten zu Leben, Werk und Rezeptionsgeschichte der Mozarts*. 2 vols., Tutzing 2004

Bauer, Günther G.: *Mozart. Glück Spiel und Leidenschaft*. Bad Honnef 2003

Bär, Carl: *Mozart. Krankheit, Tod, Begräbnis* (= Schriftenreihe der Internationalen Stiftung Mozarteum 1). 2nd edition Salzburg 1972

Becker, Max und Schickhaus, Stefan: *Wolfgang Amadeus Mozart. Chronik Bildbiografie*. Gütersloh 2005

Becker, Max (ed.): Mozart,. *Sein Leben und seine Zeit in Texten und Bildern*. Frankfurt – Leipzig 1991

Braunbehrens, Volkmar: *Mozart – Lebensbilder*. Bergisch Gladbach 2005

Braunbehrens, Volkmar: *Mozart in Wien*. Munich. 4th edition 1989

Braunbehrens, Volkmar: *Mozart. Ein Lebensbild*. Munich 1994

*Der Mozart-Erinnerungsraum in Mozarts Wohnung von 1784–1787*. Catalog of the Historisches Museum der Stadt Wien, 1953

Einstein, Alfred: *Mozart. Sein Charakter – sein Werk*. Frankfurt 2005

Elias, Norbert: *Mozart. Zur Soziologie eines Genies*. Frankfurt 2005

Fath, Rolf: *Reclams Mozart-Opernführer*. Stuttgart 2005

Geck, Martin: *Mozart. Eine Biografie*. Hamburg 2005

Gruber, Gernot: *Mozart verstehen. Ein Versuch*. Salzburg 1990

Gruber, Gernot. *Mozart und die Nachwelt*. Salzburg 1985

Hamann, Brigitte: *Nichts als Musik im Kopf. Das Leben von Wolfgang Amadeus Mozart.* Vienna 1990

Hildesheimer, Wolfgang: *Mozart.* Frankfurt a.M. 1980

Kelly, Michael: *Reminiscences.* 2 vols. London 1826

Kesting, Hanjo: *Der Musick gehorsame Tochter. Mozart und seine Librettisten.* Göttingen 2005

Klose, Dietrich (Hg.): *Zuviel Noten, lieber Mozart. Stimmen von Musikern, Dichtern und Liebhabern.* Stuttgart. 2nd edition. 2005

Knepler, Georg: *Wolfgang Amadé Mozart – Annäherungen.* Berlin 1991

Knepler, Georg:. *Wolfgang Amadé Mozart Annäherungen.* Leipzig 2005

Konrad, Ulrich: *Wolfgang Amadé Mozart. Leben, Musik, Werkbestand.* Kassel 2005

Kretschmer, Helmut: *Mozarts Spuren in Wien.* Vienna 1990

Lachmayer, Herbert; Haigermoser Theresa; Eisendle, Reinhard (eds.): *Salieri sulle tracce di Mozart.* Catalog of the Da Ponte Institute accompanying the exhibition in the Palazzo Reale. Kassel–Basel–London–New York–Prag 2004

Landon, Howard C. Robbins (ed.): *Das Mozart Kompendium. Sein Leben – seine Musik.* Munich 1991

Landon, Howard C. Robbins: *Mozart. Die Wiener Jahre 1781–1791.* Munich 1990

Landon, Howard C. Robbins: *Mozart, the Golden Years.* London 1989

Leonhart, Dorothea: *Mozart.* Zürich 2005

*Mozarts Wohnung in der Schulerstraße 1784–1787.* Catalog of the Historisches Museum der Stadt Wien, 1965

*Mozart-Wohnung (Figarohaus), Wien 1, Domgasse 5.* Catalog of the Historisches Museum der Stadt Wien, 1981

Nagel, Ivan: *Autonomie und Gnade. Über Mozarts Opern.* Munich 2005

Niemetschek, Franz Xaver: *Ich kannte Mozart. Die einzige Biografie von einem Augenzeugen.* Munich 2005

Piek, Werner: *Die Mozarts. Porträt einer Familie.* Hamburg 1998

Prochazka, Elsa: *Musikergedenkstätten in Wien, ein museologisches Konzept.* In: Wolfgang Amadeus Mozart. »Figarohaus«. Catalog of the Historisches Museum der Stadt Wien [1996]

Solomon, Maynard: *Mozart – A Life.* New York 1995

Unseld, Melanie: *Mozarts Frauen. Begegnungen in Musik und Liebe.* Reinbek bei Hamburg: Rowohlt Taschenbuch Verlag 2005

Wagner, Christoph: *Amadeus à la carte. Eine kulinarische Reise durch die Mozartzeit mit vielen leicht nachkochbaren Rezepten.* Vienna 2005

Weiss, Walter M.: *Auf den Spuren von Wolfgang Amadeus Mozart: Ein biografischer Reiseführer durch Salzburg, Prag und Wien.* Vienna 1997

Wignall, Harrison James: *In Mozart's Footsteps: A Travel Guide for Music Lovers.* New York 1991

Wolfgang Amadeus Mozart. »Figarohaus«. Catalog of the Historisches Museum der Stadt Wien [1996]. (Parts of these texts have been included in our publication).

*Zaubertöne. Mozart in Wien 1781–1791* (= 139th special exhibition of the Historisches Museum der Stadt Wien). Vienna 1990

SOME OF THE EXHIBITS
ARE ON LOAN FROM:

ADEVA Graz

akg-images, Berlin London Paris

Albertina, Vienna

Archiv der Universität Wien

Augsburg, Stadtarchiv

Bibliothèque nationale France

Bibliothèque nationale Paris

British Library, London

Château de Versailles

Deutsches Literaturarchiv Schiller-Nationalmuseum, Marbach

Deutsches Historisches Museum, Berlin

Deutsches Museum, Munich

Gabinet Rycin Biblioteki Uniwersyteckiej w Warszawie

Gesellschaft der Musikfreunde in Wien

Goethe-Museum, Anton-und-Katharina-Kippenberg-Stiftung

Großloge von Österreich

Hofmobiliendepot – Möbel Museum, Vienna

Hradec u. Opavy, Schloss

Hunterian Museum, Glasgow

Imagno

Institut für Geschichte der Medizin, Vienna

Internationale Stiftung Mozarteum (ISM) Salzburg

Internationale Stiftung Mozarteum (ISM) Bibliothek Rara, Salzburg

KirchGroup

Kunsthistorisches Museum (KHM), Vienna

Muzeum Hlavniho Mestra Prahy

National Library of Australia

Naturhistorisches Museum, Vienna (NHM)

New York Yacht Club, NYC

Österreichische Galerie Belvedere, Vienna

Österreichische Nationalbibliothek (ÖNB), Handschriften-, Autographen- und Nachlass-Sammlung

Österreichische Nationalbibliothek (ÖNB), Musiksammlung

Österreichische Nationalbibliothek (ÖNB), Kartensammlung

Österreichische Nationalbibliothek (ÖNB), Theatersammlung (Theatermuseum)

Österreichisches Freimaurermuseum, Schloss Rosenau

Österreichisches Haus-, Hof- und Staatsarchiv (ÖStA)

Royal College of Music, London

Sammlung Asenbaum

Schloss Dux

Staatsbibliothek zu Berlin

Statni Oblasti Archiv v Praze, Prag

Technisches Museum, Vienna

The New York Public Library – Photographic Services & Permission

The Saul Zaentz Company

Times Corporation, London

Universität Köln, Institut für Theaterwissenschaft

Wien Museum

Wiener Schubertbund

Wiener Stadt- und Landesbibliothek (WStLB)

Wiener Stadt- und Landesarchiv (WStLA)

As well as from various private individuals who prefer to remain anonymous.

## PARTNERS AND SUPPORTERS

PARTNERS:

WienHolding

RaiffeisenHolding NÖ-Wien

Wien Museum

WienMozart 2006

The project has been co-financed by
the European Union

SUPPORTING SPONSORS:

Gewista

Toyota Frey

Telekom Austria

OTHER SPONSORS:

Nomura

Österreichische Lotterien

Brau Union

Bösendorfer

Flughafen Wien

The visual material for "Mozart and
his Time" in the entrance hall
of the museum has been provided by
imagno.

The musical recordings for the
audioguide as well as the music
in the individual rooms have been
made available by Universal Music
and drawn from the repertoire of
Deutsche Grammophon.

PHOTOGRAPHIC CREDITS

The photographs of the exhibits
shown have been provided by the
respective institutions.

Architectural drawings:
Atelier Pichelmann (House, second
and third floors)
Lichtwitz – Büro für visuelle Kommu-
nikation / propeller z (Mozart Apartment)

Photographs of Mozart and his age
(room 3.04 and biography):
imagno

Photographs "From the 'Figarohaus'
to the Mozarthaus Vienna":
Wien Museum, Norbert Novak
Votava

Photograph of the model of the
Games Room (see pp. 72/73):
Benjamin Eichhorn
Model: Augustin Fischer

Multimedia presentations:
checkpointmedia AG

Photographs of the house:
David Peters


TEXTS

Alfred Stalzer, Ulrike Spring:
"From the 'Figarohaus' to the
Mozarthaus Vienna"
Chronology (based on the Mozart
catalog of the Historisches Museum
der Stadt Wien, 1996)
Bibliography

Alfred Stalzer, Wolfgang Kos:
"Renovation of the Building and
Installation of the Mozarthaus Vienna"

Alfred Stalzer, Joachim Riedl,
Isolde von Mersi:
Tour of the Third and Second Floors

"Großloge von Österreich":
"Mozart and the Freemasons"
(rooms 3.05 and 3.06)

Wolfgang Kos, Ulrike Spring,
Werner Hanak, Adalbert Schusser
(expert advice):
Tour of the First Floor: Mozart Apartment of the Wien Museum (based on
the Mozart catalog of the Historisches
Museum der Stadt Wien, 1996)

Concept and editing:
Alfred Stalzer
Isolde von Mersi (assistant)

MOZARTHAUS VIENNA
Domgasse 5, 1010 Vienna
Tel.: +43 (1) 512 17 91
www.mozarthausvienna.at
info@mozarthausvienna.at
Daily 10 a.m. to 8 p.m.

© 2006 Prestel Verlag
Munich · Berlin · London · New York

PRESTEL VERLAG
Königinstraße 9, 80539 Munich
Tel.: +49 (89) 38 17 09-0
Fax: +49 (89) 38 17 09-35

Prestel Publishing Ltd.
4, Bloomsbury Place
London WC1A 2QA
Tel. +44 (020) 7323-5004
Fax +44 (020) 7636-8004

Prestel Publishing
900 Broadway, Suite 603
New York, N.Y. 10003
Tel. +1 (212) 995-2720
Fax +1 (212) 995-2733
www.prestel.com

Library of Congress Cataloguing-in-
Publication Data is available; British
Library Cataloguing-in-Publication
Data. A catalogue record for this book
is available from the British Library;
Deutsche Bibliothek holds a record
of this publication in the Deutsche
Nationalbibliografie; detailed biblio-
graphical data can be found under:
http://dnb.ddb.de

Project Coordination and Editing:
Gabriele Ebbecke

Translated from the German by:
Stephen Telfer, Edinburgh
Michael Knight, Munich

Layout and Production:
Andrea Mogwitz

Origination:
David Peters, Fotostudio Otto,
Salon Iris

Printing and Binding:
Passavia Druckservice GmbH, Passau

Printed in Germany on acid-free paper

ISBN 3-7913-3617-7 (English edition)
ISBN 3-7913-3616-9 (German edition)
ISBN 3-7913-3618-5 (French edition)
ISBN 3-7913-3619-3 (Italian edition)
ISBN 3-7913-3620-7 (Japanese edition)